NATIONAL SOUTHWEST BORDER COUNTERNARCOTICS STRATEGY

Office of National Drug Control Policy

2011

Message from the Director

I am pleased to transmit the 2011 *National Southwest Border Counternarcotics Strategy*, consistent with the provisions of Section 1110 of the Office of National Drug Control Policy Reauthorization Act of 2006 (Public Law 109-469).

The 2009 *National Southwest Border Counternarcotics Strategy* focused primarily on what the U.S. Government could do to prevent the trafficking of illicit drugs across the border with Mexico, as well as the illegal outbound movement of weapons and bulk currency from the United States. Since then, Mexican President Felipe Calderon has continued his courageous campaign to break the power of the criminal organizations operating in his country. Through the Mérida Initiative and other programs, the United States is supporting Mexico's efforts in a wide range of law enforcement and judicial areas, and I am pleased to see our cooperation continue to improve. These efforts have resulted in the capture or death of numerous leaders as well as disruptions in their operations. However, Mexico continues to face high levels of violence, and our Nation—especially the four border states—continues to face significant drug- and border-related challenges, making this updated *National Southwest Border Counternarcotics Strategy* an important part of our comprehensive national response.

As a result of the changing situation on the border, the 2011 *National Southwest Border Counternarcotics Strategy* has expanded its focus beyond stemming the flow of illegal drugs, weapons, and bulk currency between the U.S. and Mexico. It also includes a "Strong Communities" chapter that directs Federal agencies to provide border communities with enhanced prevention and drug treatment assistance in this region that has borne the brunt of the consequences of the drug trade.

The Strategy is the result of an expanded consultation process which included visits to U.S. border areas, as well as to Mexico, to ensure thorough coordination with Congressional, state, local, and tribal authorities, as well as the Government of Mexico. I would like to thank the Department of Homeland Security's Office of Counternarcotics Enforcement, and the Department of Justice's Office of the Deputy Attorney General for the leadership role they played as Executive Agents in the development of this Strategy. Along with the Mérida Initiative, the Administration's Southwest Border security bill, and our national effort to reduce the demand for illegal drugs at home, the National Southwest Border Counternarcotics Strategy is a key component of our response to the threat along the border. I thank the Congress for its efforts on this issue and ask that it continue to support this critical endeavor.

R. A. Kerlikowske

R. Gil Kerlikowske
Director, Office of National Drug Control Policy

Table of Contents

Introduction 1

Chapter 1: Intelligence and Information Sharing 9

Chapter 2: At the Ports of Entry 13

Chapter 3: Between the Ports of Entry 17

Chapter 4: Air and Marine 21

Chapter 5: Investigations and Prosecutions 25

Chapter 6: Money 31

Chapter 7: Weapons 37

Chapter 8: Technology 43

Chapter 9: Strong Communities 47

Chapter 10: Cooperation with Mexico 55

Appendix A: Tunnel Strategy 59

Appendix B: Resources 67

Appendix C: Common Abbreviations 95

Introduction

"I have made securing our Southwest border a top priority since I came to office. That is why my administration has dedicated unprecedented resources and personnel to combating the transnational criminal organizations that traffic in drugs, weapons, and money, and smuggle people across the border with Mexico."

—President Barack H. Obama, August 13, 2010

Illicit trafficking across the Southwest border continues to be a chronic threat to our Nation and one of the top homeland security priorities for the United States. Transnational criminal organizations in Mexico dominate the illegal drug supply chain, taking ownership of drug shipments after they depart South America and overseeing their transportation to market and distribution throughout the United States. It is estimated that approximately 90 percent of the cocaine that is destined for U.S. markets transits the Mexico/Central America corridor. Mexico is the primary foreign source of marijuana and methamphetamine destined for U.S. markets and is also a source and transit country for heroin. Transnational criminal organizations based in Mexico dominate the U.S. drug trade—not just in border areas, but throughout much of the Nation. These organizations also control the south-bound flow of drug-related bulk currency and illegal weapons.

The U.S. Government is responding to the range of threats along both sides of the Southwest border in several ways. President Obama signed the Southwest Border Security Bill on August 13, 2010, in response to immediate threats associated with a substantial increase in violence in Mexico, which resulted from pressure placed on the cartels by Mexican authorities and inter-cartel violence. This included $600 million in supplemental funds for enhanced border protection and law enforcement activities. The President also separately authorized the temporary deployment of up to an additional 1,200 National Guard troops to the border to contribute additional capabilities and capacity to assist law enforcement agencies as a bridge to longer-term enhancements in the efforts to target illicit networks' trafficking in people, drugs, illegal weapons, money, and the violence associated with these illegal activities.[1] The Department of Homeland Security (DHS) is working to better coordinate its intra-departmental efforts, and the Administration is monitoring the situation on the border to assess how additional law enforcement and border security resources are disrupting illicit activities. These efforts are supported by our continuing partnership with Mexico through the Mérida Initiative, a multi-year program led by the Department of State (DOS) which provides over $1.4 billion in assistance to Mexico to help address the threat posed to both our nations by transnational criminal organizations. Through the end of 2010, $361.8 million in equipment and training was delivered, with an additional $500 million planned for delivery by the end of 2011.

---

1. The Departments of Homeland Security and Defense agreed to equally fund this National Guard support; however, as Congress rejected the Department of Homeland Security's reprogramming requests, the Department of Defense has funded the full cost.

Our response to the threats along the Southwest border employs unprecedented technology, personnel, and resources, and is making an impact. For the first time, DHS now has Predator Unmanned Aircraft System coverage along the entire Southwest border, from the El Centro Sector in California to the Gulf of Mexico in Texas. DHS is also improving its tactical communications systems and adding two new forward operating bases to improve coordination of border security activities. The Border Patrol increased its agents from approximately 10,000 in 2004 to over 20,700 today. The Drug Enforcement Administration (DEA) allocated nearly 29 percent of its domestic agent positions to the Southwest border, while U.S. Immigration and Customs Enforcement (ICE) increased its Federal agents on the border from 3,034 in FY 2008 to approximately 3,300 in FY 2010. National Seizure System data indicates that over the past two fiscal years Federal Law Enforcement in the Southwest border states has seized more than $108 million in illegal currency and more than 7.7 million pounds of drugs—representing increases of more than 60 percent in illegal currency seizures and more than 30 percent in illegal drug seizures compared to the previous two years. The Department of Justice (DOJ) secured a record number of extraditions from Mexico: 107 in 2009 compared to 12 in 2000 and trained over 5,400 Mexican prosecutors and investigators. Federal, state, local, tribal, and international efforts are paying off, but we recognize that our efforts must not let up.

The 2011 *National Southwest Border Counternarcotics Strategy* guides and coordinates this broad, whole-of-government effort by presenting the progress made since the 2009 *National Southwest Border Counternarcotics Strategy* and providing updated objectives and actions that respond to evolving challenges and threats. This Strategy focuses on the following strategic goal and ten strategic objectives:

Strategic Goal

Substantially reduce the flow of illicit drugs, drug proceeds, and associated instruments of violence across the Southwest border.

Strategic Objectives

1. **Enhance intelligence and information sharing capabilities and processes associated with the Southwest border**

2. **Interdict drugs, drug proceeds, and associated instruments of violence at the ports of entry along the Southwest border**

3. **Interdict drugs, drug proceeds, and associated instruments of violence between the ports of entry along the Southwest border**

4. **Interdict drugs, drug proceeds, and associated instruments of violence in the air and maritime domains along the Southwest border**

5. **Disrupt and dismantle drug trafficking organizations operating along the Southwest border.**

6. **Stem the flow of illicit proceeds across the Southwest border into Mexico**

7. **Stem the flow of illegal weapons across the Southwest border into Mexico**

8. **Provide improved counterdrug technological capabilities and capacities for drug investigation and interdiction activities along the Southwest border**

9. **Develop strong and resilient communities that resist criminal activity and promote healthy lifestyles**

10. **Enhance U.S.—Mexico cooperation on joint counterdrug efforts**

Each of this Strategy's 10 chapters addresses one of the Strategic Objectives above by providing specific details and a summary of supporting actions. Chapter 1 describes efforts to improve intelligence and information sharing. Chapters 2 and 3 focus on efforts to prevent smuggling at and between the ports of entry (POEs). Chapter 4 discusses air and marine assets utilized in interdiction efforts. Chapter 5 presents priority actions needed to support investigations and prosecutions. Chapter 6 concentrates on efforts to counter money laundering and bulk cash smuggling across the Southwest border. Chapter 7 outlines steps to combat the illegal smuggling/trafficking of weapons from the United States into Mexico. Chapter 8 advises on technology needs to advance efforts against narcotics smuggling. Chapter 9 is a new addition to the Strategy, which focuses on efforts to develop strong, resilient border communities that resist criminal activity and promote healthy lifestyles. Chapter 10 links this Strategy to our partnership with the Government of Mexico, building upon on-going cooperation and integrating efforts launched through the Mérida Initiative.

In addition to these Strategic Objectives, enhancing the Federal partnership with state, local, and tribal law enforcement agencies remains one of the major areas of emphasis in this strategy. State, local, and tribal law enforcement agencies are key players in border security efforts, particularly with regard to the south-bound flow of illegal weapons and money. In order to leverage the on-the-ground knowledge and experience of state, local, and tribal law enforcement authorities, the Office of National Drug Control Policy (ONDCP) and partner agencies conducted a four-state consultation tour of the Southwest border from August 30th through September 2nd, 2010. The input received during that tour, in addition to written input received from border region law enforcement authorities, elected officials, and stakeholder organizations, played a critical role in shaping this Strategy. Engaging state, local, and tribal law enforcement in a genuine partnership with their Federal counterparts will enable the Nation to address the threat posed by violent drug cartels in a more comprehensive manner.

The *National Southwest Border Counternarcotics Strategy* is an integrated component of the Administration's broader national drug control policy. This policy includes a renewed commitment to reduce the demand for illegal drugs at home through a balanced approach that provides increased support to prevention, treatment, and other programs. As noted in the previous edition of this Strategy, the demand for illegal drugs in the United States remains a driving factor for the threat along the border. In Chapter 9, the Strategy provides a plan tailored to the unique characteristics of the Southwest border region to further prevention and treatment efforts in border communities that have faced serious consequences from the flow of drugs, money, and weapons through the region.

This 2011 *National Southwest Border Counternarcotics Strategy* is submitted pursuant to Section 1110 of the Office of National Drug Control Policy Reauthorization Act of 2006 (Public Law 109-469). Public Law 109-469 requires that not later than 120 days after the date of enactment, and every 2 years thereafter, the Director of National Drug Control Policy shall submit to the Congress a Southwest Border Counternarcotics Strategy, and that the document shall:

1. set forth the Government's strategy for preventing the illegal trafficking of drugs across the international border between the United States and Mexico, including through ports of entry and between ports of entry on that border;

2. state the specific roles and responsibilities of the relevant National Drug Control Program agencies (as defined in Section 702(7) of the National Drug Control Policy Reauthorization Act of 1998 (21 U.S.C. 1701(7)) for implementing that strategy; and

3. identify the specific resources required to enable the relevant National Drug Control Program agencies to implement that strategy.

Public Law 109-469, Section 1110 (c) additionally mandates that the strategy incorporate specific content related to drug tunnels between the United States and Mexico including (1) a strategy to end the construction and use of tunnels and subterranean passages that cross the international border between the United States and Mexico for the purpose of illegal trafficking of drugs across such border; and (2) recommendations for criminal penalties for persons who construct or use a tunnel or subterranean passage for such a purpose. These drug tunnel requirements are addressed in Appendix A.

ONDCP will oversee the implementation of this Strategy, in coordination with the Department of Homeland Security, Office of Counternarcotics Enforcement (DHS/CNE), and the Department of Justice, Office of the Deputy Attorney General (DOJ/ODAG), through meetings of the Southwest Border Executive Steering Group (SWB ESG). This group, which includes senior leaders from the Southwest border High Intensity Drug Trafficking Areas (HIDTA) and over 20 Federal agencies involved in Southwest border security, meets several times a year to assess Strategy implementation progress, review input received from state, local, and tribal partners, and develop responses to emerging challenges. Through the SWB ESG, the Administration will work continuously to ensure Federal, state, local, tribal, and international partners are acting in concert to reduce drug-related threats along the Southwest border.

Measuring Progress on the Implementation of the National Southwest Border Counternarcotics Strategy

To ensure effective implementation of the *National Southwest Border Counternarcotics Strategy* (Strategy), it is critical to have indicators that will enable status tracking of the Strategy's implementation. Provided below are measurable indicators corresponding to the ten strategic objectives of the Strategy. While progress reports on the Strategy will include narratives highlighting successes and identifying challenges in more detail, the intent is to provide a consolidated list of indicators, one per objective, which provides a "dashboard" indicating the extent of progress in pursuing the strategic goal of the *National Southwest Border Counternarcotics Strategy*. These indicators are not comprehensive and do not reflect all that is contained within each chapter, but they do provide an "at a glance" indication of our progress in some of the most crucial areas of the Strategy. These indicators will be compared to baseline numbers as of June 2009, when the Administration's first *National Southwest Border Counternarcotics Strategy* was published.

Strategic Goal

Substantially reduce the flow of illicit drugs, drug proceeds, and associated instruments of violence across the Southwest border.

Strategic Objectives

Chapter 1: Intelligence and Information Sharing

- **Objective:** Enhance intelligence and information sharing capabilities and processes associated with the Southwest border

- **Indicator:** Number of intelligence databases relevant to the Southwest Border or counternarcotics that the following entities have access to: El Paso Intelligence Center (EPIC), Organized Crime Drug Enforcement Task Force (OCDETF) fusion centers, Southwest border HIDTAs, and state and major urban area fusion centers in the Southwest border region

Chapter 2: At the Ports of Entry

- **Objective:** Interdict drugs, drug proceeds, and associated instruments of violence at the ports of entry along the Southwest border

- **Indicator:** All seizures at Southwest border ports of entry in the following categories:

Marijuana	Cocaine	Heroin	Methamphetamine	Bulk Currency	Firearms

Chapter 3: Between the Ports of Entry (POEs)

- **Objective:** Interdict drugs, drug proceeds, and associated instruments of violence between the ports of entry along the Southwest border

- **Indicator:** Seizures in Southwest border sectors (not counting at the POEs) in the following categories:

Marijuana	Cocaine	Heroin	Methamphetamine	Bulk Currency	Firearms

Chapter 4: Air and Marine

- **Objective:** Interdict drugs, drug proceeds, and associated illicit activities in the air and maritime domains along the Southwest border

- **Indicator:** Seizures along the Southwest border and maritime approaches by Customs and Border Protection's Office of Air and Marine (CBP/OAM) and the U.S. Coast Guard (USCG) in the following categories:

Marijuana	Cocaine	Heroin	Methamphetamine	Bulk Currency	Firearms

Chapter 5: Investigations and Prosecutions

- **Objective:** Disrupt and dismantle drug trafficking organizations operating along the Southwest border

- **Indicator:** Number of Attorney General's Mexico-based Consolidated Priority Organization Target (CPOT) linked drug trafficking organizations disrupted or dismantled having a Southwest border-nexus

Chapter 6: Money

- **Objective:** Stem the flow of illicit proceeds across the Southwest border into Mexico

- **Indicator:** Number of Mexico-based CPOT-linked primary money laundering organizations (PMLOs) disrupted or dismantled having a Southwest border-nexus

Chapter 7: Weapons

- **Objective:** Stem the flow of illegal weapons across the Southwest border into Mexico.

- **Indicator:** Number of firearms trafficking/smuggling seizures with a nexus to Mexico.

Chapter 8: Technology

- **Objective:** Provide improved technological capabilities and capacities for drug investigation and interdiction activities along the Southwest border

- **Indicator:** Percentage of the Department of Homeland Security's borders and maritime security program milestones that are met, as established in the fiscal year budget execution plan

Chapter 9: Strong Communities

- **Objective:** Develop strong, resilient communities that resist criminal activity and promote healthy lifestyles

- **Indicator:** Past 30-day use of alcohol, tobacco, and marijuana in middle and high school students in Drug Free Communities along the southwest border

Chapter 10: Cooperation with Mexico

- **Objective:** Enhance U.S.—Mexico cooperation on joint counterdrug efforts

- **Indicator:** Number of Mexico-based CPOT-linked drug trafficking organizations disrupted or dismantled with the assistance of Government of Mexico authorities

Chapter 1: Intelligence and Information Sharing

> **Chapter 1 Strategic Objective**
>
> **Enhance intelligence and information sharing capabilities and processes associated with the Southwest border**

Background

Since the 2009 Strategy was released, law enforcement agencies and the Intelligence Community have continued to strengthen cooperative efforts to address an expanding range of interrelated challenges on the Southwest border, from drug and human smuggling into the United States, to the transit of arms and bulk cash from the United States to Mexico, to the associated violence in border communities. These initiatives have led to substantial improvements in the combined intelligence capabilities of Federal, state, local, tribal, and international partners along the Southwest border. Progress in information sharing has paralleled this increase in capabilities, as improved technology and new information-sharing protocols have expanded collection, analysis, and dissemination capabilities between and among partners at all levels. Successful initiatives include:

- Assignment of additional intelligence analysts, operations specialists, reports officers and collection requirements managers to EPIC and Southwest border fusion centers

- The establishment of the Border Intelligence Fusion Section (BIFS) at EPIC as an all-source, all-threats intelligence section to support tactical and operational efforts with fused intelligence and analysis

- Installation of the Homeland Secure Data Network (HSDN) at fusion centers

- Major enhancements to the EPIC Open Connectivity program

- Agreement on and movement toward a reliance on a Common Intelligence Picture for all law enforcement personnel along the Southwest border

As the Administration moves to implement its vision for a 21st century border, accurate, actionable, and timely information and intelligence will become increasingly important to creating a border that enables the secure, efficient, rapid, and lawful movement of goods and people.

Over the next few years, Intelligence Community and law enforcement agencies with Southwest border responsibilities will build on the strides they have already made. They will enhance their capacities to integrate multiple sources of information and intelligence into fused analyses at the tactical, operational, and strategic level. They will improve the timeliness of the dissemination of products and produce a Common Intelligence Picture. They will continue to work to ensure analysis incorporates all available information sources, and that it supports the operational needs of law enforcement and other border operations personnel seeking to identify trafficking patterns, develop investigative leads, and interdict illegal goods.

This chapter addresses specific intelligence programs and activities to enhance support to investigations and operations along the Southwest border. The supporting actions are designed to improve the quality and timeliness of intelligence relating to the Southwest border, and to enhance support to Federal, state, local, and tribal efforts along the land, air, and maritime domains of the Southwest border. The intelligence efforts in this Strategy will be aligned with and incorporate other national intelligence efforts along the Southwest border and broader national counternarcotics activities, particularly those efforts coordinated by the Director of National Intelligence, ONDCP/HIDTA, DEA, ICE, Department of Defense (DOD), non-Federal, and international partners. The results will better inform both operational and strategic decision making in combating transnational threats.

Supporting Actions

1. **Enhance coordination and collaboration on intelligence collection, tactical and strategic analysis, and dissemination among the Intelligence Community, law enforcement agencies, and other government entities**

A. Enhance the Southwest Border Intelligence Integration Working Group (SWBIIWG) to oversee and facilitate implementation of all actions in this chapter
The SWBIIWG, co-chaired by the DEA/Intelligence Division, and the DHS/Office of Intelligence and Analysis, has been re-established to coordinate implementation of intelligence initiatives contained in this Strategy. Working Group members include representatives from all Federal agencies/entities with a role in providing counterdrug intelligence support for the Southwest border. The SWBIIWG will continue to address specific intelligence integration objectives, activities, or supporting actions, and will, as necessary, collaborate with and seek assistance from other existing coordination groups. **Action: DOJ/DEA, DHS/I&A, DOJ/FBI, DOJ/ATF, DOJ/NDIC, DOD/DIA, DOD/NGB, DOD/USNORTHCOM, DHS/ICE, DHS/CBP, DHS/USCG, EPIC, DOJ/OCDETF, ODNI, ONDCP, CIA/CNC, Treasury**

B. Enhance coordination of existing intelligence requirements processes among law enforcement and Intelligence Community organizations, as well as those of non-Federal partners
Agencies will continue to expand efforts to coordinate and integrate intelligence requirements to increase efficiency, improve productivity, and reduce strain on the system. The DOJ and DHS have significantly improved the Request for Information (RFI) processes and the Collections and Requirements Management Unit (CRMU) at EPIC. Coordination of intelligence requirements will be further enhanced by the establishment of the interagency Border Intelligence Fusion Section (BIFS) at EPIC and CBP's Intelligence Operations Coordination Centers, which will pool border-related intelligence resources from existing intelligence centers. Agencies will also build capabilities to prioritize intelligence requirements and integrate state, local, and tribal intelligence needs, while continuing to develop coordination mechanisms for requirements processes and systems. **Action: DHS/I&A, DOJ/DEA/EPIC, DOJ/NDIC, DOJ/FBI, DHS/ICE, DHS/CBP, DOJ/ATF, DOD/USNORTHCOM, DHS/USCG, ONDCP/HIDTA-ISC, ODNI, Treasury**

C. Enhance coordination and integration of Southwest border-related intelligence collection programs and activities

It is essential that intelligence collection programs and activities be carried out in a coordinated and cohesive manner, driven by priorities and measured for performance. Since the 2009 Strategy was released, DOJ/DEA and DHS/CBP have established a post-seizure reporting system at EPIC to more fully exploit Federal, state, and local reporting. DOJ/DEA and DHS/CBP have also enhanced the License Plate Reader (LPR) program by broadening the availability of LPR data and will continue to improve access to and coordination of LPR data. DHS/CBP, DOJ/DEA, and the U.S. Marshals Service Tactical Operations Group (USMS/TOG) will also continue to improve coordination of Law Enforcement Technical Collection (LETC) programs with DHS/ICE. The coordination of border-related intelligence collection efforts will continue to improve with the development of tools and programs such as the Unified Collection Plan, consolidated all-source collection management tools, and a Coast Guard-led interagency maritime biometrics program. **Action: DOJ/DEA, DHS/I&A, DOJ/FBI, DOJ/USMS/TOG, DHS/ICE, DOJ/ATF, DHS/CBP, DOJ/NDIC, ODNI, ONDCP/HIDTA, DHS/USCG**

D. Empower the Deputy National Intelligence Officer (D/NIO) for Counterdrug Analysis to coordinate intelligence assessment production through the interagency Anti-Drug Intelligence Community Team (ADICT) and DHS/I&A

Law enforcement, Intelligence Community, and other agencies will share annual production plans to the extent practicable, and the D/NIO will chair regular meetings of ADICT and the interagency to discuss short-term production plans and identify opportunities for interagency collaboration. **Action: D/NIO, ADICT, DHS/I&A**

E. Enhance activities to link intelligence efforts and products to operational needs and capabilities

Greater emphasis will be placed on ensuring intelligence products contain operational links that add value to interdiction and investigative activities. Efforts that closely link intelligence and operations, such as the BIFS and Gatekeeper program at EPIC, the DHS supported ACTT, the Federal Bureau of Investigation's (FBI) Southwest Intelligence Group, and HIDTA's Domestic Highway Enforcement Initiative, will be sustained and improved. CBP has established an Intelligence and Operations Coordination Center in Tucson, AZ, and may establish additional centers along the Southwest border. DOJ will continue OCDETF efforts, and ICE will advance its Border Enforcement Security Task Force (BEST) program through enhancements to personnel and capabilities in fusion center locations across the Southwest border region. Efforts to exploit and share seizure and investigative information for tactically relevant intelligence will be enhanced by the development of all-source intelligence fusion capabilities. Agencies will need to assign additional intelligence analysts to frontline operational organizations to support these on-going efforts to better link intelligence to operations. **Action: DHS/I&A, DHS/ICE, DHS/CBP, DHS/USCG, DOD/DIA, DOD/USNORTHCOM/JTF-N, NSA, DOJ/ATF, DOJ/DEA, EPIC, DOJ/FBI, DOJ/NDIC, DOJ/OCDETF, ONDCP/HIDTA, Treasury**

2. **Institutionalize programs and technological infrastructure to enable timely intelligence and information sharing collaboration**

A. Enhance intelligence coordination and sharing among Federal law enforcement, Department of Defense, international partners, and Intelligence Community elements and centers

The Interdiction Committee (TIC), EPIC, and the SWBIIWG will coordinate drafting and clearance of interagency information-sharing protocols, in accordance with the Executive Order on Classified National Security Information Programs for state, local, tribal, and private sector entities. Agencies will build on efforts to coordinate and share Common Operating Picture and Common Intelligence Picture capabilities, and will consider concepts that could virtually link centers on the Southwest border with the Joint Interagency Task Forces and other national centers. The SWBIIWG will continue to work to identify specific methods to improve intelligence coordination, information sharing, collaboration, and the integration of systems and processes. **Action: EPIC, DHS/I&A, DOJ/DEA, DOJ/ATF, DOJ/FBI, DOJ/OCDETF, DHS/ICE, DHS/CBP, DHS/USCG, DOD/DIA, DOD/USNORTHCOM/JTF-N, ADICT, ONDCP/HIDTA-ISC, TIC, Treasury**

B. Enhance intelligence coordination and sharing between Federal agencies/entities and state, local, and tribal entities with responsibility for the Southwest border

Efforts to enhance information-sharing processes, procedures, and technology among Federal, state, local, and tribal partners will continue to expand the scope, quality, and timeliness of actionable and strategic information. Institutionalizing this progress will require updating existing information-sharing agreements and, where necessary, entering into new agreements. Initiatives will focus on enhancing and better coordinating existing activities such as EPIC, state and major urban area fusion centers, BESTs, and HIDTAs along the Southwest border, as well as the systems used for information sharing. Interagency partners will also work to ensure full participation in the Consolidated Counterdrug Database (CCDB), which includes information on where, when, and how individual drug trafficking events took place; the response of interdiction forces to those events; the outcome of an event; and the type and quantity of drugs involved. Agencies also will continue efforts to sanitize and disseminate information and intelligence derived from classified reporting and law enforcement investigations, through the expansion of initiatives such as the DHS and DEA "Reports Officer" programs that have been successful in extracting and disseminating intelligence and information derived from operational and investigative activities. **Action: DHS/I&A, EPIC, DOJ/DEA, DHS/ICE, DHS/CBP, DHS/USCG, DOJ/ATF, DOJ/NDIC, DOD/USNORTHCOM/JTF-N, ONDCP/HIDTA-ISC, RISS, DOJ/OCDETF, TIC, Treasury/FinCEN**

C. Enhance coordination of intelligence sharing with Mexico, including information provided to and received from Mexican agencies

The U.S. Government will continually explore further opportunities for analytic collaboration, information sharing, and other collaborative efforts with Mexico's Center for Investigation and National Security (CISEN) and its other intelligence and law enforcement entities. The SWBIIWG will lead the development of guidelines for sharing operational and strategic information and intelligence with Mexican counterparts. **Action: EPIC, DHS/I&A, DOJ/DEA, DOJ/ATF, DOJ/FBI, DOJ/NDIC, DOJ/USMS, DHS/ICE, DHS/CBP, DHS/USCG, DOD/DIA, DOD/USNORTHCOM/JTF-N, Treasury, DOS**

Chapter 2: At the Ports of Entry

> **Chapter 2 Strategic Objective**
>
> **Interdict drugs, drug proceeds, and associated instruments of violence at the ports of entry along the Southwest border**

Background

Although U.S. border security and law enforcement personnel have made significant progress in seizing drugs and other contraband at our Nation's Southwest border POEs, challenges remain. Drug traffickers alter both the methods and timing of their operations in response to border interdiction activities. In order to achieve the goal of protecting our borders, the United States continues to expand its defenses at the POEs.

Since March 2009, CBP has increased its emphasis on outbound enforcement activity, establishing a new policy and program office to address outbound infrastructure challenges, staffing needs, inspection equipment improvements, canine resources, and automation enhancements. This new Outbound Division focuses on developing and implementing security programs that focus on interdicting illicit proceeds, firearms, and ammunition from entering Mexico while also facilitating the secure and efficient flow of legitimate trade and travel.

While technology, improved resources, and enhanced communication can bolster narcotics interdiction efforts, improved targeting of border threats, in advance of their arrival, is essential. These efforts can be realized by implementing a coordinated bilateral and multi-agency approach to sharing passenger and cargo data.

Supporting Actions

1. **Use state-of-the-art detection technology, resources, and training to interdict drugs and other contraband**

A. Expand use of drug detection technology by frontline officers

Frontline border officers and agents utilize an array of detection technology as a "force multiplier" to maximize their efficiency and effectiveness. CBP uses large-scale X-ray and gamma ray imaging systems to perform thorough examinations of cargo without having to resort to the costly, time-consuming process of unloading cargo for manual searches or intrusive examination of conveyances by methods such as drilling or dismantling. Currently, CBP has a total of 137 large-scale imaging systems deployed at and between the POEs on the Southwest border. CBP also employs low energy mobile imaging systems to scan outbound vehicles for contraband. Currently, a total of 52 low-energy mobile imaging systems are deployed to our POEs along the Southwest border. Both programs will continue to expand in FY11. **Action: DHS/CBP, DHS/S&T, ONDCP/CTAC**

B. Increase canine unit capabilities for drug detection at POEs

Canines are regarded as one of the most effective and time-tested tools available for drug detection. Additional canine units at POEs along the Southwest border significantly enhance CBP counternarcotics screening and detection capabilities in both the vehicle-processing and cargo-processing environments and significantly decrease cargo and vehicle examination times. Currently, CBP has 341 canine teams deployed along the Southwest border, and will continue to monitor the need for more teams in FY 11. **Action: DHS/CBP**

C. Disrupt surveillance operations conducted by drug trafficking organizations at ports of entry

Drug trafficking organizations engage in a number of counter surveillance collection activities, including the use of "spotters" at POEs on the U.S. and Mexican sides of the border. The United States and Mexico will work together to coordinate operations aimed at disrupting intelligence collection activities conducted by drug trafficking organizations. **Action: DHS/CBP, DHS/I&A, DHS/ICE, DOJ/FBI, DOJ/DEA**

2. Improve targeting of border threats

A. Increase use of advance information

Interdiction agencies have improved the use, analysis, and dissemination of advance information, such as passenger and cargo data, to identify and target border threats. One notable initiative of the National Targeting Center—Cargo involves firearms shipments being examined at the U.S. port of export to verify contents and quantities. Confirmation is obtained from Mexican authorities regarding the shipments, orders and expected delivery to ensure the legitimacy of the shipments and reduce the possibility of diversion. Additional efforts to leverage advance information are being taken by organizations such as ICE; the Embassy Intelligence Fusion Center; Joint Interagency Task Force South; Joint Task Force North; and Mexican law enforcement partners. **Action: DHS/CBP, DHS/US-VISIT, DOJ/OCDETF, DHS/ICE, DHS/S&T, DHS/USCG, DOJ/FBI, DOJ/DEA, DOS, EPIC, DOJ/NDIC, DOD, ONDCP/HIDTA, DOJ/ATF, IC, TREASURY**

B. Improve and integrate border databases

DHS is improving targeting and analysis by integrating existing databases and enhancing CBP's existing rules-based targeting system. CBP's Automated Targeting System (ATS) is now fully deployed for use at land POEs and the system will be enhanced to include updates, entity recognition, stolen vehicles, and the ability for users to create lookouts. Modifications will also be made to the Automated Export System (AES) to alert users of possible fraud or stolen firearms or vehicles. It will also provide export reporting capabilities. The U.S. Government will continue the development and expansion of such systems as CBP's Automated Commercial Environment, EPIC's Open Connectivity Project, the OCDETF Fusion Center database, and the National Drug Intelligence Center (NDIC) Document and Media Exploitation Real-Time Analytical Intelligence Database (RAID) application. In addition, DHS will work with individual HIDTAs and other applicable agencies to link POE and Border Patrol LPR databases with other interagency LPR systems. **Action: DHS/CBP, DHS/US-VISIT, DOJ/OCDETF, DHS/ICE, DHS/S&T, DOD, DOS, EPIC, DOJ/NDIC, ONDCP/HIDTA**

C. Enhance identity management and document security

The security of the Southwest border can be significantly enhanced through information sharing and biometric solutions for criminal alien cross-border identity management. Due to the continued influx of Special Interest Aliens (SIA) into Mexico, U.S. representatives have been receiving biographic and biometric information from Mexico's CISEN. CBP Mexico has been entering this information into the targeting framework and is forwarding this information to all the Border Intelligence Centers as well as the National Targeting Center-Passenger. However, the quality of the scanned fingerprints must increase to be compatible with US-VISIT. CBP is currently working with Mexico's Secretaria de Gobernacion (SEGOB) to install electronic fingerprint scanners at immigration detention centers in Mexico. **Action: DOS, DHS/ICE, DHS/US-VISIT, DHS/CBP, DHS/CIS, DHS/S&T, EPIC**

D. Enhance use of trade information

The United States will work with foreign governments and the trade community to prescreen, target, and inspect shipments and containers that pose a potential risk before they arrive at U.S. or Mexican POEs. Through programs like the voluntary Customs-Trade Partnership Against Terrorism, DHS will partner with the trade community to develop secure cargo containers, to establish minimum standards for cargo security, and to secure global supply chains. At the national level, the Coast Guard Intelligence Coordination Center's (ICC) Coastwatch program screens Notices of Arrival and Notices of Departure submitted by commercial vessels desiring to enter and depart the United States. The focus of the screening is to identify persons, vessels, or cargo that might pose a risk to national security. The Coast Guard recently relocated Coastwatch to the National Targeting Center-Passenger (NTC-P) and incorporated CBP's Automated Targeting System to streamline maritime screening, enable real time database checks, and allow for the development of scenario based targeting rule sets. Coastwatch screening will also incorporate the Automated Commercial Environment, which will provide three dimensional stowage plans that can be reviewed prior to boarding the vessel. CBP continues to provide training and technical assistance to Mexican Customs as it establishes its own industry partnership supply chain security program. **Action: DHS/CBP, DHS/ICE, DHS/USCG, DOS**

E. Increase focus on cargo containers

CBP has developed the Container Security Initiative and the Secure Freight Initiative to identify high-risk cargo overseas before it arrives in the United States. The U.S. Government will continue to work with the Government of Mexico to improve the exchange of information about cargo that could contain high-risk material destined for the Southwest border. **Action: DHS/CBP, DHS/ICE, DHS/USCG, DOS, EPIC**

F. Promote the development of intelligence-based targeting

CBP's Field Operations Intelligence program will provide support to CBP inspection and border enforcement personnel in disrupting the flow of drugs through the collection and analysis of all-source information and the dissemination of intelligence to the appropriate components. Activities such as Operation Buckstop, which screens outbound travelers and their personal effects for currency, and Operation Cashnet, which interdicts bulk currency exported in cargo shipments, will be continued at the POEs. **Action: DOJ/OCDETF, DHS/ICE, DOJ/DEA, EPIC, TREASURY/OFAC, DOS, IC**

3. Improve capability to interdict southbound currency/firearms

A. Improve infrastructure at the POEs

CBP has initiated efforts to provide temporary and re-locatable infrastructure for up to 21 crossings along the Southwest border. The infrastructure improvements include: canopies for operations under inclement weather, improved lighting for night operations, traffic control devices for officer safety, connectivity to CBP's automated databases, and vehicle blocking devices for those attempting to flee prosecution. Construction is expected to commence in spring 2011. **Action: DHS/CBP**

B. Use license plate data at the POEs

LPRs are recognized as a fundamental component of all technical solutions to provide advance information to CBP officers to support pulse and surge operations focused on travelers, conveyances, and cargo leaving the United States. However, several CBP outbound lanes still have not been outfitted with LPRs. Current funding is being utilized to ensure a variety of LPR solutions are tested, evaluated, and verified to meet CBP's operational (and constrained) outbound environment. Site surveys have been conducted for the remaining outbound lanes to ensure the sites are suitable for LPR installation in the near future. **Action: DHS/CBP, DOJ/DEA, DHS/ICE, DOJ/ATF, DHS/S&T, ONDCP/CTAC**

Chapter 3: Between the Ports of Entry

> **Chapter 3 Strategic Objective**
>
> **Interdict drugs, drug proceeds, and associated instruments of violence between the ports of entry along the Southwest border**

Background

In addition to the ports of entry, the Southwest border includes thousands of miles of open desert, rugged mountains, the Rio Grande River, and the maritime transit lanes into California and Texas. This vast and diverse range of environments presents opportunities for terrorists, drug traffickers, and human smugglers to cross into the United States undetected. The linkages between drug trafficking organizations operating in Mexico, at or near the Southwest border, and human smuggling groups are well documented. In addition, the routes and methods of existing smuggling organizations could potentially be utilized to transport terrorists or weapons of mass destruction across the border. Enhancing U.S. counternarcotics efforts along the Southwest border strengthens our all-threats approach to border security.

Expanding capabilities and increasing coordination and partnerships is the path forward to increase border security. BEST teams along the Southwest border will continue to unite the efforts of Federal, state, local, and foreign law enforcement partners to leverage a comprehensive approach toward the investigation of transnational criminal organizations. Operation Stonegarden (OPSG) funds will be utilized to enhance cooperation and coordination among Federal, state, local, and tribal law enforcement agencies in a joint mission to secure the borders along routes of ingress and egress and on tribal lands adjacent to the border. OPSG funds are also utilized to increase operational capabilities of state, local, and tribal law enforcement agencies, promoting a layered, coordinated approach to law enforcement with a variety of patrol activities.

Supporting Actions

1. **Expand the operational capabilities of U.S. personnel at or near the border**

A. Enhance patrol and interdiction capabilities

Technology, infrastructure, personnel, and intelligence are critical elements of effective border interdiction efforts. Utilizing the proper mix of these elements is essential to the U.S. Border Patrol's operations to detect, identify, classify, and respond to all illegal cross-border activities. A multi-layered defense provides the best enforcement posture for detecting and seizing illegal drugs. This multi-layered defense should include enhancements to U.S. Border Patrol checkpoints, including the improvement of facilities, the expansion of canine capabilities, the use of non-intrusive inspection equipment, and the leveraging of other resources that improve detection capabilities near checkpoints. CBP has added hundreds of miles of tactical infrastructure in the form of fencing and vehicle barriers, and deployed new technology platforms such as mobile surveillance systems with ground surveillance radar. The U.S. Border Patrol will also expand its staffing to more than 21,000 agents by the end of 2011. **Action: CBP, ICE, USMS, DOD**

B. Enhance capability to assess suspects

The U.S. Government will improve the ability of border personnel to assess the threat posed by individuals apprehended between POEs through better coordination and information sharing among Federal, state, local, and tribal law enforcement and intelligence communities. Methods of collecting information from those housed at detention facilities will be further developed and improved. All Border Patrol stations now have connectivity to the Automated Biometrics Identification System (IDENT) and the Integrated Automated Fingerprint Identification System (IAFIS), and efforts will be made to provide additional mobile capabilities for these systems so agents can access them in the field. Border law enforcement personnel will expand the use of resources at EPIC, NDIC, and the OCDETF Fusion Center. **Action: DHS/CBP, DHS/ICE, DHS/I&A, DOJ/DEA, EPIC, DOJ/FBI, DOJ/NDIC, DOJ/USMS, DOS, DOD, DOJ/OCDETF**

2. Improve coordinated operations and partnerships on the Southwest border

A. Enhance capability of task force initiatives

Multi-agency task force initiatives have been developed to enhance information sharing and increase the effectiveness of law enforcement operations along the Southwest border. For example, DHS has 11 of its 21 BEST teams located on the Southwest border. The BESTs include participation from ICE, CBP Office of Field Operations, U.S. Border Patrol, DEA, Bureau of Alcohol, Tobacco, Firearms and Explosives (ATF), the U.S. Attorney's Office, the Coast Guard, key state and local law enforcement agencies, and, in some locations, Mexican law enforcement liaisons. Additionally, OCDETF Southwest Border Strike Forces conduct joint operations targeting drug traffickers and money launderers operating in their regions. Further efforts will be made to promote smoother collaboration and to increase cost-effectiveness by co-locating coordination centers, such as the HIDTAs and state and local fusion centers. **Action: DHS/ ICE, DHS/CBP, DOJ/DEA, DHS/USCG, DOJ/FBI, DOS, Treasury, ONDCP/Southwest Border HIDTA, DOJ/OCDETF, DOJ/USMS, DOD/USNORTHCOM/JTF-N, IC**

B. Upgrade collaboration with non-Federal and international partners

The Federal Government will enhance partnerships with state, local, and tribal law enforcement agencies through outreach programs. Agencies will expand the use of enforcement, working through existing programs to include Southwest border HIDTAs, BESTs, and Operation Stonegarden when possible. Initiatives such as Operation Streamline and Operation Texas Hold 'Em are currently being evaluated for expansion to additional areas along the Southwest border. The Border Patrol will continue to utilize International Liaison Units to encourage collaboration between U.S. and Mexican law enforcement agencies to fight cross-border criminal organizations through information and intelligence sharing.

The Border Patrol will work to facilitate new partnerships, improve relationships, and cultivate trust throughout the Native American tribes which have a nexus to the United States border. The United States Border Patrol will continue to work with Federal land management agencies to include: Bureau of Land Management (BLM), National Park Service (NPS), U.S. Fish and Wildlife Service (USFWS), Bureau of Indian Affairs (BIA), and U.S. Forest Service (USFS). ICE will also work closely with tribal nation partners including the Shadow Wolves, DHS' Native American law enforcement officers based on the Tohono

O'Odham Nation in southern Arizona. **Action: DHS/CBP, DHS/ICE, DOJ/DEA, DOJ/FBI, DOA, DOI, DOI/ BLM, DOI/NPS, DOI/USFWS, USDA/USFS, DOJ/ATF, DOJ/USMS, DOJ/OCDETF, ONDCP/Southwest Border HIDTA**

C. Enhance interagency planning processes and apply best practices

Law enforcement leaders will establish regular Southwest border interdiction planning sessions. Existing law enforcement coordination efforts will be reviewed and expanded through the identification and application of best practices. An interagency working group will be established or dedicated as a single point of contact to collect, develop, and publish lessons learned from previous interagency counterdrug operations. Through ACTT, DHS, ICE, CBP, and USCG are conducting operations and planning together and are improving collaboration with other Federal and non-Federal agencies. **Action: DHS/CBP, DHS/ ICE, DHS/USCG, DOJ/DEA, ONDCP/Southwest Border HIDTA, DOI/BLM, DOI/NPS, DOI/USFWS, USDA/USFS, DOD, DOJ/ATF, DOJ/OCDETF**

D. Upgrade and standardize communications on the Southwest border

CBP continues to modernize current communications systems to provide greater range, more security, and increased capability for incorporating emerging changes in technology to meet the needs of Federal, state, local, and tribal law enforcement. CBP continues to establish communications interoperability among Southwest border law enforcement personnel, which will contribute to the greater success of interdiction, enforcement, and investigative operations. The U.S. Border Patrol maintains a Memorandum of Understanding (MOU) with the Department of the Interior and the Department of Agriculture (USDA) regarding radio interoperability. The U.S. Coast Guard is coordinating an Information Sharing Agreement with CBP for the purpose of enhancing communication interoperability using the National Law Enforcement Communications Center. **Action: DHS/CBP, DOI, DHS/USCG, USDA**

Chapter 4: Air and Marine

> **Chapter 4 Strategic Objective**
>
> **Interdict drugs, drug proceeds, and associated illicit activities in the air and maritime domains along the Southwest border**

Background

As a direct result of increased detection and interdiction of more traditional smuggling conveyances, ultra-light aircraft (ULAs) have been employed along the Southwest border by transnational criminal organizations. While the emerging ULA threat adds a new dimension to drug movement across the land border into the United States, go-fast vessels (including lanchas and pangas) remain the primary maritime means for smuggling activity. Since the 2009 Strategy was published, the U.S. Government has made enormous strides toward attaining more comprehensive all-domain (air, land, maritime) awareness through the acquisition and fielding of new detection and monitoring technologies, information technologies, and the strategic placement of aviation and maritime assets to deny illicit smuggling attempts along the Southwest border.

Close bi-lateral cooperation with Mexico will facilitate improved awareness of the air, land, and maritime threats bound for the United States, and thereby continue to help improve the U.S. Government's ability to respond to those threats. Technologies that help create all-domain awareness continue to be instrumental in the U.S. Government's effort to gain and maintain effective control of the Southwest border. As the lead Federal maritime and air border security components, the Coast Guard and CBP work with other Federal, state, local, and international partners to help deny transnational criminal organizations the use of the air and maritime approaches to the Southwest border. This approach includes disrupting the maritime movement of bulk illegal drugs in the drug transit zone before they have a chance to reach Central America, Mexico, and the United States.

Supporting Actions

1. **Continue planned enhancements of the air and marine presence along the Southwest border**

A. Optimize detection and response capabilities

CBP/OAM has increased the number of air and marine assets along the Southwest border to enhance detection and response capabilities. Using fixed wing, rotary wing, and unmanned aerial surveillance (UAS) assets along with maritime assets, OAM provides the specialized detection and response capabilities necessary to increase border security in the harsh climate and vast expanses of the Southwest border. Data gathered from these assets feed into the CBP Air and Marine Operations Center (AMOC), which provides real-time information on detected suspect targets to responders at the Federal, state, and local levels. USMS/TOG uses fixed wing aerial surveillance assets along with sophisticated technical surveillance equipment to enhance the capabilities of Federal, state, and local law enforcement agencies responsible for covering the Southwest border. National Guard aviation reconnaissance operations, operating pursuant to approved State drug interdiction and counterdrug activities plans, continue to provide invaluable information, including full-motion video, to Federal, state, and local law enforcement agencies. The recently enhanced air and maritime presence along the Southwest border by both CBP and Coast Guard will be maintained. **Action: DHS/USCG, DHS/CBP, DHS/ICE, DOD, DOJ/USMS/TOG**

Joint Interagency Operations in the Maritime Domain

The Joint Harbor Operations Center (JHOC) in San Diego, California is an example of the evolution of joint interagency operations to optimize detection and response. The JHOC is a multi-agency command center with a mandate to coordinate maritime law enforcement operations within its area of responsibility. The JHOC is manned with USCG, CBP, and U.S. Navy patrol watch standers. The Maritime Unified Command is chaired jointly by USCG and CBP, and includes representatives from the Maritime Task Force (which is an ICE-centric DHS/DOJ task force), U.S. Navy Third Fleet, Joint Task Force-North, the California National Guard, and local law enforcement.

The JHOC is instrumental in implementing Operation BAJA OLEADA in the San Diego area of responsibility. This long-standing operation provides a continuous maritime detection, monitoring, interdiction, and apprehension presence via cutter and small boat response and JHOC maritime patrol aircraft from USCG, OAM, and DOD. Similarly, Operation GULF WATCH in the Corpus Christi area of responsibility ensures continuous counter-drug operations in the Gulf of Mexico. The USCG works with CBP and JTF-North utilizing intelligence to integrate ground, air, and surface operations. These on-going operations help maintain an effective maritime presence in the Pacific and Gulf of Mexico border regions.

---

2. **Enhance bilateral air and maritime cooperation**

A. Expand liaison and information sharing activities with Mexico

The Government of Mexico has personnel currently serving at the AMOC that coordinate Mexican government responses to suspect air targets in conjunction with the American Embassy in Mexico City. Procedures currently exist to assist Mexican aviation and ground interdiction forces in apprehending suspect air targets. OAM and ICE have both continued to maintain a liaison presence within Mexico's coordination center, and the U.S. and Mexican Governments continue to explore the possibility of sharing radar data feeds in order to improve the bilateral air picture through integration of northern Mexico radar feeds into the AMOC.

In the maritime domain along the U.S. Southwest border, the Coast Guard, along with the U.S. Northern Command, Canada, and Mexico's Secretaria de Marina (SEMAR), have developed standard operating procedures for operations center-to-operations center communications through the North American Security Initiative. The procedures substantially improve command and control interoperability and place designated Coast Guard and Navy centers into an approved communications relationship for multi-mission patrol and boarding operations. These procedures also advance the process of integrating the diplomatic and operational channels for boarding requests with Mexico, which has already resulted in more efficient operations. To improve communications between Coast Guard, DOD, and SEMAR, as well as Central American countries, each agency participates in the Partner Nation Network (PNN), which employs the Cooperating National Information Exchange System (CNIES) to rapidly disseminate Law Enforcement operational and tactical law enforcement information. **Action: DHS/USCG, DHS/CBP, DHS/ICE, DOD, EPIC, DOS**

In pursuit of enhancing bilateral information sharing and cooperation, OAM has permanent and temporary personnel assigned to the Information Analysis Center (IAC) at the U.S. Embassy in Mexico City, Mexico. These OAM team members contribute to closer bilateral cooperation with Mexico, increasing the potential to reveal more about the air, land, and maritime threats bound for the United States and to improve our ability to respond to those threats. This center develops actionable intelligence which is shared among the agencies that participate in the program and between the Government of Mexico and the United States.

Additionally, AMOC has historically engaged in close coordination with the Government of Mexico and with Mexican law enforcement personnel. In order to enhance the air domain picture, develop intelligence, and resolve conflicts with aircraft originating in GOM airspace, the AMOC houses one liaison from the Secretaria de Seguridad Publica (SSP). Currently, AMOC is actively pursuing the development of near- and long-term Mexico communication opportunities. In the very near future, an additional liaison from Procuradura General de la República (PGR) is expected. Discussions are also underway for the introduction of a liaison from Portal de la Secretaría de la Defensa Nacional (SEDENA). Current and future Government of Mexico liaisons will provide the vital bilateral information sharing necessary to enhance national security along the Southwest border.

3. Collect comprehensive information on the air and maritime threat

A. Modernize sensors and other collection mechanisms

To help improve low-level air detection and monitoring along the Southwest border, DOD and DHS continue to coordinate the testing, evaluation, and employment of suitable surveillance technology. The DOD-owned Tethered Aerostat Radar System (TARS) is an effective tool to detect low-flying aircraft, maritime, and land traffic at the border and between the ports of entry. An effort to integrate DOD portable radar systems will further optimize the air picture. The portable radar arrays will enhance AMOC detection and monitoring capability by fusing data with those from FAA radars and TARS to provide AMOC operators an improved, persistent, and sustained air picture that is capable of tracking any airborne threat, including the growing use of ULAs.

CBP also has acquired and deployed mobile surveillance systems (MSS) in select areas of the Southwest border. These MSS units include a radar system and video camera mounted on a rugged truck that can be driven to tactical areas of high risk along the border. The Coast Guard has employed deployable multi-sensor DOD detection technology in both the Pacific and Gulf maritime regions to enhance the operating picture and better identify, track, and intercept maritime targets of interest in support of surge operations. Agencies should continue to develop and utilize all available means for detection and tracking of suspect air and maritime contacts, and improve information sharing to enhance Southwest border domain awareness, including improved technology and mechanisms to share information with other Federal, state, and local partners. **Action: DHS/CBP, DHS/USCG, DHS/S&T, DOD**

Combating the Emerging Ultra Light Aircraft (ULA) Threat: the detection of ULAs is made difficult due to their low radar profile, small size, and unconventional flight characteristics. Recognizing a current technology gap in detecting ULAs, DHS Office of Technology Innovation and Acquisition allotted $15 million in Border Security Fencing, Infrastructure and Technologies funding toward technologies to detect ULAs. The funding will provide up to 400 miles of coverage using overlapping technologies which, when interlaced with current AMOC detection efforts, will provide a more effective ULA detection capability.

B. Establish a common air domain awareness governance structure

The Department of Defense, the Department of Transportation, and the DHS have been engaged in both individual and collective efforts to address policy, resource, and capabilities issues affecting national air domain awareness. A whole-of-government approach will be required as the Federal Aviation Administration pursues its next generation air traffic control solution and as issues arise concerning the capabilities needed to secure the national airspace system. To that end, the interagency will accelerate current efforts to establish a national air domain awareness governance structure empowered to bring all the affected departments and agencies together to coordinate policy issues, and propose new or re-allocated authorities. **Action: DHS/CBP, DOD/NORAD, DHS/USCG, NGB, FAA, EPIC, DOD/JIATF-S**

4. Improve coordination with state, local, and tribal counterparts

A. Enhance coordination of state, local, and tribal border security and law enforcement activities along the Southwest border

Agencies should develop and maintain frameworks that address the coordination, integration, deconfliction, and synchronization of Federal, state, local, and tribal border security and law enforcement activities along the Southwest border. One such framework is ACTT, a DHS initiative to build a cooperative effort between the many agencies operating along the Southwest border. The ACTT divides the Southwest border into four corridors: Southern California, Arizona, New Mexico/West Texas, and Southeast Texas. Each is projected to have an ACTT modeled on the integrated structure and coordination at the Joint Harbor Operations Center in San Diego. The ACTT will involve a coordinated approach across all domains utilizing the capabilities of regional air and land assets with the AMOC and maritime assets through the JHOC or similar maritime unified commands where applicable. DHS is also pursuing the development of another framework in the form of the BIFS. The BIFS will enhance existing capabilities within EPIC to provide a strong focus on support to Federal, state, local, and tribal law enforcement agencies with responsibilities along the Southwest border, leveraging EPIC resources, and coordinating Southwest border-related intelligence sharing through collaboration with all agencies at EPIC. To better maximize the effectiveness of law enforcement responses, OAM reaches out to local law enforcement agencies to provide information on OAM capabilities and available support. **Action: DHS/CBP, DHS/USCG, ONDCP/Southwest border HIDTA, EPIC**

Chapter 5: Investigations and Prosecutions

> **Chapter 5 Strategic Objective**
>
> **Disrupt and dismantle drug trafficking organizations operating along the Southwest border**

Background

Today, seven major cartels operating throughout Mexico control the flow of drugs across the Southwest border: the Arellano-Felix Cartel (Tijuana Cartel), the Gulf Cartel, the Los Zetas Cartel, the Juarez Cartel, the Sinaloa Cartel, the Beltran-Leyva Cartel, and the La Familia Michoacán Cartel. Pressure is building on these cartels as a result of the aggressive counter-drug efforts of President Felipe Calderon's administration in Mexico and increasing competition with one another. However, violence in Mexico has reached alarming levels, with over 8,700 drug-related homicides occurring in the country during 2009, and over 34,000 reported homicides since President Calderón took office in December 2006. The reach of these cartels does not end inside of Mexico or on the Southwest border. Cells operating on behalf of these cartels have influence in over 300 U.S. cities, and their presence has been documented in the Caribbean, Central America, and South America, as well as Africa, Australia, and Europe. It is now more imperative than ever to focus U.S. and Mexican law enforcement efforts on disrupting and dismantling these criminal organizations.

Targeting and attacking criminal organizations through investigations and prosecutions is critical to an effective counternarcotics strategy on the Southwest border. Given the magnitude of the threat, U.S. law enforcement and intelligence agencies must explore ways to enhance their capacities to undertake or assist such investigation and prosecution efforts. U.S. and Mexican law enforcement and intelligence communities must also closely coordinate their efforts to disrupt and dismantle criminal organizations responsible for the movement of illicit drugs, firearms, and drug proceeds across the Southwest border by building strong cases against these organizations and bringing cartel leaders to justice.

Supporting Actions

1. **Broaden the presence and function of U.S. law enforcement liaisons in Mexico**

A. Expedite expansion of U.S. law enforcement liaison presence in Mexico
Placing expert U.S. personnel where the cartels are operating will enable closer collaboration with Mexican law enforcement partners. Due to the vast geographic area of Mexico and the direct impact that drug trafficking and related criminal activity in Mexico have on the United States, U.S. law enforcement agencies must, with the consent of the Government of Mexico, work to increase their liaison presence in key Mexican cities along the U.S.-Mexico border and in other locations in order to support the investigation and prosecution of transnational criminal organizations. **Action: DOJ, DHS, DOS, DOJ/USMS/TOG, Treasury/OFAC**

B. Use joint and coordinated efforts among U.S. law enforcement agencies to disrupt and dismantle drug trafficking organizations operating along the Southwest border

Improved investigative collaboration and coordination between key U.S. law enforcement agencies, task forces, and HIDTA offices will increase the ability of the U.S. and Mexican governments to attack the financial infrastructures and commercial operations of major trafficking organizations, while also enhancing criminal investigations and prosecutions. In addition, continued utilization of the multi-agency and operational support centers, such as the Special Operations Division, OCDETF Fusion Center, ICE-Bulk Cash Smuggling Center, EPIC, FBI Southwest Intelligence Group, Financial Crimes Enforcement Network (FinCEN), and other national and local de-confliction centers, will ensure complete investigations and prosecutions. **Action: DHS/ICE, Treasury/IRS, Treasury/OFAC, DOJ/DEA, DOJ/FBI, DOJ/ USMS, Treasury/FinCEN, DHS/USCG**

2. **Increase the investigative, prosecutorial and judicial resources dedicated to cases relating to Mexico and the Southwest border**

A. Increase the Federal, state, tribal and local law enforcement resources dedicated to Southwest border-related investigations

The sophisticated Mexico-based transnational criminal organizations responsible for supplying most of our Nation's illegal drug market also engage in a variety of other crimes, including extortion, torture, murder, corruption of public officials, harboring of fugitives, kidnapping, human smuggling, money laundering, and firearms trafficking. Attacking these organized, multi-faceted criminal enterprises in their entirety requires the active and coordinated participation of multiple Federal, state, tribal, and local agencies with sufficient expertise and resources to support all phases of the investigations. Although in recent years the hiring of Federal interdiction agents deployed to the Southwest border has increased substantially, and many agencies have been able to temporarily re-deploy existing investigative agent resources, there is still a pressing need for experienced investigators to keep pace with the enormously high caseload of complex and time-intensive investigations. Increasing investigative resources will help law enforcement maintain pace with these growing caseloads. **Action: DOJ, DHS**

B. Increase the capacities of U.S. Attorneys Offices to handle Southwest border drug investigations and prosecutions

Prosecutors on the Southwest border currently handle staggering caseloads which will only increase with intensified security efforts. A comprehensive strategy must increase the capacities of the U.S. Attorneys' Offices to handle Southwest border drug smuggling and trafficking investigations and prosecutions by ensuring sufficient OCDETF and non-OCDETF Assistant U.S. Attorney (AUSA) resources. Successful and timely prosecutions also require comprehensive support resources including paralegals, clerical staff, equipment, office space, and document translation services. The Border Security Act of August 2010 partially alleviated the problem of declining prosecutorial resources by authorizing new OCDETF and non-OCDETF funding for increased numbers of AUSAs to handle Southwest border work. However, this funding needs to be annualized to ensure a sustained USAO capacity to handle the growing caseload along the Southwest border. **Action: DOJ**

C. Increase the capacities of other criminal justice components to support Southwest border drug investigations and prosecutions

Intensified efforts in targeting, interdiction, investigation, and prosecution of Southwest border drug cases necessarily have an impact on other criminal justice system components. To handle the increased number of investigations and prosecutions, more support is required for judges, pretrial services and probation officers, Assistant Federal Public Defenders and court-appointed defense attorneys, Deputy U.S. Marshals, and Federal corrections officers. In addition, there must be adequate detention facilities and bed space for both pre-trial detainees and convicted prisoners. The increased numbers of complex investigations will necessitate support for the Department of Justice's Office of Enforcement Operations, which handles applications for judicially authorized Title III wiretaps; the Office of International Affairs, which handles requests for foreign evidence and extraditions; the Narcotics and Dangerous Drugs Section (NDDS), which prosecutes major drug trafficking organizations operating along and across the Southwest border; the multi-agency Special Operations Division (SOD), which coordinates complex multi-jurisdiction, multi-nation investigations; and the Department of State's Office of the Legal Advisor, which handles extradition matters. **Action: DOJ, DOS**

D. Develop prosecution policies to address special issues regarding juveniles and kidnappings arising in drug trafficking cases

Drug trafficking organizations operating in the Southwest border region have been using juveniles on an increasing basis, often in roles as couriers or lookouts, hoping they will not be prosecuted by either Federal or state authorities. The Federal system is often ill-equipped to handle juvenile defendants, and state authorities frequently release such offenders, due to strained resources or the low prospects for successful prosecution. Federal and state prosecutors should work together to develop policies on prosecuting juveniles who violate Federal drug laws and those who utilize juveniles to commit Federal drug crimes. In addition, Federal and state prosecutors should be encouraged to place more emphasis on cases involving kidnappings related to drug trafficking activity. **Action: DOJ**

E. Enhance the capacities of investigative agencies and U.S. Attorneys Offices to dismantle the financial infrastructure of Southwest border drug trafficking organizations

In order to disrupt and dismantle the most significant drug trafficking organizations contributing to the Southwest border threat, investigations and prosecutions must attack the entire financial infrastructure of the targeted organizations and destroy their ability to operate. As part of this goal, law enforcement should seek to improve financial investigations that follow bulk cash interdictions. In addition, OCDETF member agencies will continue to train and assist state and local law enforcement at all levels of experience to gain valuable intelligence for investigation development following bulk cash seizures. **Action: DOJ, DHS/ICE, DOJ/NDIC, DOJ/DEA, DOS, IC, Treasury**

F. Modify Federal grant rules to increase utility for state and local law enforcement

Federal grant programs currently allocate funds based upon violent crime rates and other criteria that do not fully reflect the threat faced by communities along the Southwest border. Year-to-year grant funding should be expanded as appropriate to allow local agencies to spend funds over a longer period of time to facilitate planning and more effective use of grant dollars. Federal agencies should also seek to modify grant funding processes to permit local agencies to use Federal grants for new hiring, in addition to funding overtime. **Action: DOJ, DHS, ONDCP**

G. Maximize use of the Kingpin Act

The Foreign Narcotics Kingpin Designation Act (Kingpin Act) may be used to prosecute U.S. persons involved in activities such as arms trafficking, bulk cash smuggling, or other activities related to international narcotics trafficking. U.S. law enforcement will continue to coordinate efforts with the Treasury Department's Office of Foreign Assets Control (OFAC) in order to increase OFAC's ability to attack financial infrastructures and commercial networks of major drug trafficking organizations, and to enhance criminal investigations and prosecutions. Further, law enforcement agencies and U.S. Attorneys' Offices should consider referring to OFAC those cases where Kingpin Act violations may warrant a civil penalty. **Action: Treasury/OFAC, DOJ**

3. Increase judicial cooperation with Mexico

A. Utilize Mérida Initiative activities and other established programs to build cooperation

The Mérida Initiative includes several programs to improve cooperation between U.S. and Mexican counterparts, including through programs related to prosecutorial capacity building, judicial exchanges, and enhancing investigative capacities. Implementation of these programs will increase the capacity for complex investigations and prosecutions on both sides of the border against narcotics trafficking and related arms smuggling/trafficking, money laundering, and corruption. New training initiatives will be developed as circumstances evolve. In addition, U.S. Government components engaged in Mérida Initiative activities should provide regular updates on those activities to law enforcement agencies along the Southwest border. **Action: DOS, DHS, DOJ/OPDAT, DOJ/USMS, Treasury/OFAC, Treasury/OTA**

B. Expand bilateral enforcement and prosecution efforts with Mexico

The Controlled Substances Program (CSP) and Illicit Drug Program (IDP) were developed by ICE and CBP with Mexico's PGR and initiated in an effort to deter criminal organizations operating on both sides of the border from utilizing the ports of entry for smuggling. The programs have fostered a stronger U.S. partnership with Mexican law enforcement and heightened collaboration with Mexican prosecutorial agencies with the goal of applying simultaneous investigative and prosecutorial pressure on both sides of the border. Originally implemented as a pilot program in Nogales, Arizona in October 2009, the CSP created a bilateral enforcement effort to combat the smuggling of controlled substances. The success of the initial CSP program led the PGR and ICE to start the IDP in El Paso, Texas, in 2010. Opportunities to expand both initiatives to new sites to enhance bilateral cooperation will be explored. **Action: DHS/ICE, DHS/CBP, DOJ/DEA, DOS**

4. Attack corruption involving domestic public officials along the Southwest border

A. Conduct integrity awareness training for U.S. law enforcement agencies working along the Southwest border

Agencies will conduct and enhance integrity awareness training for the Southwest border law enforcement workforce to ensure each employee is aware of the responsibility to report allegations of misconduct. This training also will reinforce core values in employees and thereby assist in preventing corruption in the workforce. **Action: DHS/ICE, DOJ/FBI, DHS/CBP, DOJ/DEA, DOJ/ATF, Department OIGs, ONDCP/HIDTA**

B. Increase the investigative focus on public corruption

Public corruption undermines faith and confidence in government, eroding trust in institutions upon which the Nation's democratic system is based. Corruption not only facilitates the activities of violent criminal organizations that traffic drugs, firearms, and illegal proceeds across the U.S.-Mexico border, but it also makes the United States vulnerable to terrorist attacks through the potential importation of dangerous contraband or the illegal entry of criminals, terrorists, and foreign intelligence officers. Investigating, prosecuting, and deterring corruption on all levels along the U.S. borders is vital to combating transnational organized crime and protecting national security. **Action: DHS/ICE, DOJ/FBI, DHS/ CBP, DOJ/DEA, DOJ/ATF, Department OIGs, ONDCP/HIDTA**

5. **Proactively address foreign official corruption that supports drug trafficking and related crimes**

A. Support the Department of State's anti-kleptocracy program by denying access to the United States for foreign officials suspected of corruption

Combating corruption is a foreign policy priority for the United States, as corruption facilitates virtually all transnational illicit activities, from drug trafficking to terrorist finance. Presidential Proclamation 7750 allows the United States to deny entry on the basis of corruption, even in the absence of a conviction. This denial may also extend to family members if certain conditions are met. Information supplied by law enforcement agencies to DOS, as well as information gathered by State from other sources, can be used to effectuate visa denials of current or former foreign officials. The Departments of State and Justice will work to ensure this proclamation is effectively applied. **Action: DOS, DOJ/DEA, Treasury/ IRS, DHS/I&A, DOJ/NDIC, ONDCP, DHS/CBP, DHS/ICE, DOJ/FBI, DOJ/ATF, IC**

Chapter 6: Money

Background

Mexican transnational criminal organizations remain the dominant source of supply to the illegal U.S. drug market and continue to use the Southwest border as their primary route for expatriating illicit drug proceeds. Strict compliance with the Bank Secrecy Act by U.S. financial institutions deters these criminal groups from initially placing illegal profits directly into the U.S. financial system, while also creating an evidentiary trail for law enforcement to follow in investigations and in tracking proceeds of crime. According to NDIC, Mexican and Colombian drug trafficking organizations annually generate, remove, and launder billions of dollars in wholesale distribution proceeds, much of which is believed to be smuggled in bulk out of the United States through the Southwest border.

U.S. law enforcement has documented that bulk cash fuels Mexican transnational criminal organizations as well as their illicit drug suppliers in South America, through an elaborate money laundering network. Numerous U.S. law enforcement investigations and analyses of currency flows between the United States and Mexico have confirmed this method of moving U.S.–generated drug proceeds. However, as efforts to interdict bulk cash have improved and Mexican restrictions serve to lessen the attractiveness of U.S. currency in Mexico, criminal organizations may have turned to alternative methods to launder illicit proceeds. Thus, there is a need to increase industry, regulatory, and law enforcement vigilance against criminal abuse both of traditional cross-border transmission channels, such as the use of money services businesses, and emerging types of electronic payment devices.

Since 2009, Federal, state, local, and tribal agencies have improved information sharing and increased training on bulk cash smuggling and other money laundering methods employed by drug traffickers. A number of studies and assessments have also enhanced our understanding of the illicit drug proceeds movement phenomenon. Moreover, a Congressional amendment to the money laundering statute in mid-2009 remedied a significant legal loophole, thereby providing law enforcement with another important tool in its anti-money laundering arsenal.

The success of U.S. law enforcement efforts hinges on close collaboration with Mexican counterparts, given the transnational nature of drug trafficking organizations. The extent to which Mexican criminal organizations continue to smuggle U.S. bulk cash into Mexico may be influenced by Mexico's recent implementation of regulations restricting the amount of U.S. cash that Mexican financial institutions can accept from their customers. U.S. law enforcement will need to closely monitor new money laundering trends that may result from this development. Regulatory measures should be coordinated to mitigate criminal abuse of financial transactions, while still allowing legitimate economic activity. Meanwhile, efforts are also already well underway to increase coordination with the Government of Mexico on money laundering prosecutions and asset forfeiture matters.

Supporting Actions

1. Stem the flow of outbound bulk cash smuggling

A. Enhance OCDETF operations along the Southwest border to target bulk cash movements

Efforts must be focused on the coordinated and strategic use of asset forfeiture and prosecutions, under the appropriate money laundering and/or bulk currency smuggling statutes, as well as the application of all other strategic and tactical assets to prevent the cross-border movement of illicit proceeds. U.S. law enforcement agencies will support this effort through the specific targeting of bulk cash smuggling activities across the Southwest border. Targeting of these criminal organizations should be brought under the auspices of the OCDETF program whenever possible, in order to identify and dismantle the organizations moving bulk cash across the border. **Action: DOJ, DOJ/DEA, Treasury, DHS/ICE, DOJ/OCDETF, EPIC**

B. Rapidly share bulk currency seizure information

Federal, state, local, and tribal agencies all collect and maintain separate repositories of information relating to bulk currency seizures. Some of this information is subsequently voluntarily shared with EPIC for inclusion in the National Seizure System or with ICE's Bulk Cash Smuggling Center (BCSC) for inclusion in the TECS database (formerly the Treasury Enforcement Communications System). ICE has begun developing a data link in order to automatically exchange information between the National Seizure System and TECS, which should reconcile information collected by BCSC and EPIC. Once this is accomplished, the subsequent data will establish a baseline for improving the rapid sharing of currency seizure data among Federal, state, local, and tribal agencies. **Action: DHS/ICE, DOJ, EPIC, DHS/CBP, DOJ/DEA, DHS/USCG, DOJ/FBI, ONDCP/HIDTA**

C. Coordinate Federal bulk cash concealment detection training

DEA, CBP, and ICE have each instituted bulk currency initiatives, which include analyzing and communicating new and emerging concealment and detection techniques in order to enhance south-bound interdiction efforts at ports of exit, as well as the training of state and local officers in concealment "trap" detection, methods of courier debriefing, and guidance on pertinent evidence identification. To avoid duplication of efforts, each agency that provides bulk cash concealment training should verify whether or not potential training participants may have already received bulk cash concealment detection training and then certify those individuals who do receive training. The certification and verification process should be undertaken by agency training coordinators. **Action: DHS/ICE, DOJ/DEA, EPIC, DHS/CBP, NGB, Treasury/IRS, ONDCP/HIDTA**

D. Enhance bulk currency interdiction capacities

U.S. law enforcement must increase its capabilities to interdict illicit proceeds along U.S. highways, at and between POEs, in the maritime domain, and at checkpoints. CBP and DEA have begun to enhance their out-bound targeting capabilities through the use of license plate readers, wireless handheld devices and automated targeting systems. FinCEN will work with law enforcement to develop capacities for raising awareness of out-bound Currency and Monetary Instrument Report (CMIR) requirements among international travelers. The Treasury Executive Office of Asset Forfeiture (TEOAF) and the Department of Justice's Asset Forfeiture program will continue to support the establishment of more Federal task forces and initiatives that further enhance investigations targeting the smuggling of bulk cash out of the United States. Mexico's newly implemented south-bound inspection program should also facilitate greater interdiction of bulk currency and illegal weapons flowing from the United States into Mexico. **Action: Treasury/FinCEN, DHS/CBP, DOJ/DEA, DHS/ICE, DHS/USCG, EPIC, DOS**

E. Increase interior enforcement targeting of bulk cash

U.S. law enforcement has identified primary origination points throughout the United States, where illicit drug proceeds are consolidated prior to being moved to the Southwest border, and then de-consolidated prior to being smuggled across the border. The identification of 'stash houses' at both consolidation and distribution cities identified in the U.S.-Mexico Bi-national Criminal Proceeds Study should be a priority of U.S. law enforcement. The HIDTA Domestic Highway Enforcement initiative should continue to expand and enhance efforts to target and interdict illicit bulk currency transiting our highways. Coordinated efforts between Federal, state, local, and tribal authorities

> **Deconfliction between interdiction and investigative agencies**
>
> Local deconfliction centers, such as Safe Net in New York, the Miami NINJAs, and LA Clear in Los Angeles, exist to ensure officer safety, coordination, and information sharing between interdictors and investigators. These centers are key players in identifying targets/organizations that are under investigation by one or more local, state, or Federal agencies.

are needed to best exploit the intelligence gleaned from highway interdictions, seizures of bulk cash, and CMIRs. Seizure and forfeiture of these funds should not be viewed as the end game, but rather the beginning of an investigation. All efforts need to be made to connect bulk cash to the drug trafficking organizations that generate it. **Action: DOJ/DEA, DHS/ICE, DOJ/NDIC, Treasury/IRS, DOJ/OCDETF, ONDCP/HIDTA, EPIC**

F. Update laws to counter bulk cash courier activities

In 2008, the United States Supreme Court decided Cuellar v. United States, reversing the money laundering conviction of a bulk cash courier. In Cuellar, the Court held that a conviction under the concealment prong of the international money laundering statute, 18 U.S.C. § 1956(a)(2)(B)(i), requires proof that a purpose of transporting the funds across the border was to conceal or disguise the nature, location, source, ownership, or control of the money. The Court stated that it was not enough to show the funds were transported in a secretive or clandestine manner, but it must also prove that the person transporting the funds knew the purpose of the concealment. The Administration has drafted a legislative fix that clarifies the issue and eliminates the language from the statute that caused the Supreme Court to reverse Cuellar's conviction. The Administration will continue to work with Congress to introduce and pass this legislation. **Action: DOJ**

2. **Identify, investigate, and prosecute the illegal use—and strengthen safeguards against the abuse—of money services businesses and electronic payment devices**

A. Target the illicit use of money services businesses (MSBs)

U.S. law enforcement agencies are targeting the illicit use of MSBs based in both the United States and Mexico, and efforts should continue to identify, investigate, and prosecute the illegal use of MSBs, structuring violations, and illegal use of electronic payment devices. Additionally, Federal and state regulators will continue to promote compliance with anti-money laundering regulations and to identify and mitigate vulnerabilities to money laundering and terrorist financing. Federal agencies should continue to coordinate efforts to exploit Suspicious Activity Reports (SARs) and other relevant data pointing to the use of MSBs as illicit conduits, including collaboration with the Southwest Border Alliance, USAO-led SAR Review Teams, and IRS-CI's Title 31 SAR Review Task Forces. Efforts should also be made to ensure compliance by all money transmitters and appropriate civil and criminal enforcement against unlicensed money transmitters, including those on tribal lands. If a law enforcement agency identifies an unregistered/unlicensed MSB, including those operating on tribal lands, the agency should consider referral to FinCEN for civil money penalties, or targeted outreach and follow-up, in addition to criminal prosecution. **Action: Treasury/FinCEN, Treasury/IRS, DOJ, DHS/ICE, EPIC**

> **Southwest Border Anti-Money Laundering Alliance**
>
> The Alliance was created in February 2010 through an agreement between Western Union and the four border states (Arizona, California, New Mexico, and Texas). The purpose of the Alliance is to facilitate increased cooperation, collaboration, and information sharing on investigations and prosecutions of money laundering, weapons smuggling, and related criminal activity. Funding for the initiative was provided by Western Union, as part of a settlement agreement it entered into with the Arizona Attorney General's Office.

B. Share financial investigative information and intelligence through the OCDETF Fusion Center

The OCDETF Fusion Center (OFC) provides access to investigative drug and financial intelligence possessed by all the OCDETF member agencies, as well as other agencies such as NDIC, FinCEN, and the national Intelligence Community. Combining all of this intelligence in one location helps to identify and attack drug trafficking organizations and their financing. **Action: DOJ, DOJ/NDIC, DOJ/DEA, DOJ/FBI, Treasury/FinCEN, Treasury/IRS, Treasury/OFAC, DOJ/OCDETF, DHS/ICE, EPIC**

C. Target the illicit use of electronic payment devices and cross-border wire transfers

U.S. law enforcement and regulatory agencies need to monitor evolving trends in money laundering, such as the conversion of cash through stored value devices, electronic payment devices, and online services. According to a 2010 report by the Financial Action Task Force (FATF) on new payment methods, there is evidence of criminal organizations using these methods for cross-border transactions. An effective regulatory compliance framework must be developed with emerging industries in the United States to ensure that U.S. anti-money laundering controls are implemented to effectively monitor the domestic purchase of these devices and subsequent financial transactions, and to make records available for criminal investigations. FinCEN recently published Notices of Proposed Rulemaking outlining new requirements for U.S. providers and sellers of prepaid access (including devices like plastic cards and mobile phones), as well as requirements for banks and money services businesses to report certain cross-border electronic transmittals of funds (CBETF) to FinCEN. Establishing a centralized database of CBETF will greatly assist law enforcement in detecting and investigating the financial activities of transnational drug cartels. **Action: Treasury/FinCEN, DHS/ICE, DOJ/DEA, DOJ/NDIC, DOJ/AFMLS**

3. Emphasize the application of targeted financial sanctions

A. Coordinate with the Department of Treasury's Office of Foreign Assets Control to disrupt and dismantle drug trafficking operations along the Southwest border

OFAC continues to aggressively target individuals and entities as specially designated narcotics traffickers pursuant to the Kingpin Act, including those found to be tied to the Arrellano Felix Organization, the Beltran Leyva Organization, La Familia Michoacana, Juarez Cartel, Gulf Cartel, Los Zetas, and Sinaloa Cartel. Improved investigative collaboration and coordination between OFAC and key U.S. law enforcement agencies, task forces, and HIDTA offices will increase OFAC's ability to attack financial infrastructures and commercial networks of major drug trafficking organizations, while also enhancing criminal investigations and prosecutions. **Action: Treasury/OFAC, DOJ, DOS, DOJ/DEA, DHS/ICE**

4. Enhance and utilize bilateral mechanisms.

A. Continue intelligence sharing and joint strategic projects with financial intelligence units

FinCEN and its Mexican financial intelligence unit (FIU) counterpart, the Unidad de Inteligencia Financiera (UIF), have increased their tactical- and strategic-level collaboration based on the reciprocal sharing of relevant financial data available to FinCEN and the UIF, to include joint examination of cross-border currency flows. FinCEN will also work with other FIUs in the region to establish information-sharing arrangements based on its experience working with the UIF. **Action: Treasury/FinCEN**

B. Increase coordination with Mexico on anti-money laundering regulatory efforts, international tax administration, and financial crime

FinCEN is increasing collaboration with Mexican banking regulators, including the National Banking and Securities Commission (CNBV), to share information on anti-money laundering requirements and compliance in order to strengthen the defenses of both U.S. and Mexican financial institutions against money laundering. In addition, the IRS Office of International Operations added a deputy attaché to the Mexico City post of duty to increase effectiveness in identifying emerging trends and supporting complex matters associated with international tax administration and financial crime. **Action: Treasury, Treasury/FinCEN, Treasury/IRS**

C. Increase coordination with Mexico on money laundering prosecutions and asset forfeiture matters

Both U.S. and Mexican authorities have expressed a strong commitment for using financial crimes enforcement, particularly forfeiture, to attack drug trafficking and related criminal organizations operating along the U.S.-Mexico border. In support of these goals, and working to support these bi-lateral objectives, DOJ's Asset Forfeiture and Money Laundering Section (AFMLS) continues to work closely with Mexico's PGR and SSP, to disrupt the flow of illicit proceeds back to criminal organizations. **Action: DOJ/AFMLS, Treasury**

5. **Improve statistical measures for assessing the money laundering threat**

A. Exploit and augment existing information to continue to assess money laundering vulnerabilities and measure effectiveness in combating money laundering, including analyzing the impact of regulatory efforts by Mexico

Following implementation of recent Mexican regulations restricting U.S. dollar cash transactions in Mexico, U.S. law enforcement should work closely with domestic and international partners to monitor shifts in money laundering activity and to establish strategies to counter the efforts of the cartels to find new methods for laundering illicit proceeds. The integration and analysis of financial data and law enforcement field reporting will assist law enforcement entities in their efforts to better measure the effectiveness of law enforcement and regulatory efforts to combat money laundering. **Action: Treasury, DOJ, DHS/ICE, DOJ/DEA, DOJ/NDIC**

Chapter 7: Weapons

> **Chapter 7 Strategic Objective**
>
> **Stem the flow of illegal weapons across the Southwest border into Mexico**

Background

The National Drug Intelligence Center continues to assess that Mexican drug trafficking organizations are the primary participants in, and beneficiaries of, firearms trafficking along the U.S.-Mexico border. The level of violence on the Mexico side of the border has continued to escalate, as the TCOs battle for control of drug trafficking routes. These organizations require a constant supply of firearms and ammunition to defend their territory, eliminate rivals, enforce business dealings, challenge government operations, and control organization members. This, in turn, has resulted in the proliferation of U.S.-based illegal firearms and explosives smuggling/trafficking schemes operated by individuals, gangs, drug trafficking organizations, and other criminal groups seeking to capitalize on the growing demand. ATF trace statistics show that weapons recovered in Mexico are purchased in almost every state in the United States, with the top five source states being Texas, California, Arizona, New Mexico, and Florida.

Illegally trafficked weapons from the United States are primarily transported overland into Mexico using the same routes and methods employed when smuggling bulk cash south and drugs north. Within the United States, TCOs typically rely on "straw purchasers"—a person who can legally purchase a firearm but will not be the true possessor of the weapon—to acquire firearms at gun shops, gun shows, and pawnshops. These organizations also use associations with U.S.-based prison and street gangs to facilitate the smuggling of firearms and explosives across the border. Intelligence derived from criminal investigations clearly indicates that U.S.-based street gangs are involved in both the receipt of narcotics from TCOs and the smuggling of weapons to them. The increase in gang involvement in the illicit trafficking of narcotics, humans, and firearms has the potential to increase Southwest border violence, while contributing to the profitability and growth of international gangs such as MS-13, Latin Kings, and Mexican Mafia.

Critical steps have been taken to increase the capabilities of ATF to identify, disrupt, and dismantle the organized efforts to traffic firearms from the United States to Mexico. In September of 2010, Mexico's Attorney General signed an MOU to trace seized firearms through ATF's Spanish eTrace. In total, approximately 200 Mexican law enforcement personnel will receive training and access to Spanish eTrace. This effort will enable the Mexican government to begin a comprehensive firearms tracing program that will analyze trace data and assist them in identifying trafficking routes, trends, patterns, and sources responsible for the illegal flow of firearms from the United States into Mexico.

In addition, ATF and ICE have formalized a partnership to promote coordinated law enforcement efforts both nationally and internationally through the collaborative use of both agencies' investigative authorities. By working as partners under the newly signed MOU, ATF and ICE will advance the fight against the domestic and international trafficking of firearms, ammunition, and explosives.

Supporting Actions

1. Improve intelligence and information sharing relating to illegal weapons trafficking

A. Facilitate U.S. Government interagency intelligence sharing

U.S. law enforcement organizations and intelligence agencies operate a variety of intelligence collection and analysis programs that are directly or indirectly related to weapons smuggling. DOD provides analytical support to some of these programs with regard to captured military weapons and ordnance. In order to provide better operational access and utility to law enforcement agencies, the U.S. Government will capitalize upon the existing law enforcement interagency intelligence center at EPIC. EPIC continues to enable rapid sharing of intelligence derived from U.S. law enforcement and Government of Mexico illicit weapons seizures. **Action: DOJ/DEA, DOJ/ATF, DOD, DHS/ICE**

B. Enhance programs at EPIC targeting illegal weapons smuggling/trafficking

ATF's Project Gunrunner utilizes the EPIC Gun Desk as the focal point for the collection, analysis, and dissemination of investigative leads derived from Federal, state, local, and international law enforcement agencies. This enforcement effort extends beyond the immediate border states and will support investigative and enforcement efforts in Mexico through assistance and cooperative interaction with Mexican authorities. ATF, through the newly created EPIC Firearms and Explosives Trafficking Intelligence Unit (FETIU), disseminates intelligence bulletins to law enforcement agencies across the United States that relate to trafficking patterns, recent seizures, as well as suspect tactics and techniques for concealing south-bound weapons. ATF seeks to increase staffing at the FETIU through the incorporation of partner agencies in 2011. **Action: DOJ, DOJ/ATF, DHS/ICE**

C. Continue to employ programs to rapidly share weapons seizure information among U.S. law enforcement agencies

Law enforcement organizations have a variety of intelligence collection capabilities and programs which are either directly or indirectly related to information on illicit weapons smuggling/trafficking. Such resources must be utilized in a coordinated and cohesive manner. ICE intelligence personnel and ATF FETIU located at EPIC collect and maintain information relating to weapons seizures using TECS, the National Tracing Center, Violent Crime Analysis Branch, the U.S. Bomb Data Center, and eTrace. The Gun Desk receives CBP-compiled weapons seizure data monthly for interagency post seizure analysis. This relationship affords CBP and ATF the ability to jointly develop actionable intelligence to support Project Gunrunner and associated border interdiction efforts. Based upon current interagency agreements, sharing weapons seizure information would disseminate relevant firearms intelligence to appropriate agencies and jurisdictions for better coordination of intelligence and investigative activity. **Action: DOJ/ATF, DHS/CBP, DHS/ICE**

D. Use military-to-military and military support to foreign civil law enforcement training and engagement to improve intelligence on captured weapons while building capacity for effective weapons and munitions accountability

U.S. law enforcement agencies will work with DOD to include information sharing as a topic for discussion during military-to-military engagement opportunities with Mexico and Central America to support cooperation in areas such as tracing captured weapons. DOD will recommend that counternarcotics training and engagement activities conducted by the Combatant Commands include building capacity in accounting for and securing military arms and ammunition. This is especially important regarding military-type weapons and ordnance sought by drug cartels and gangs. **Action: DOD**

> **2. Increase the interdiction of illegal weapons shipments to Mexico**

A. Expand intelligence-driven interdiction of illicit weapons shipments destined for Mexico through multi-agency investigative efforts

A primary focus of the Southwest border BESTs is to combat transnational criminal organizations trafficking weapons into Mexico from the United States and the violence associated with their activities. As part of this initiative, DHS and the Government of Mexico have partnered in bilateral interdiction, investigation, and intelligence sharing activities to identify, disrupt, and dismantle criminal networks engaged in weapons smuggling/trafficking. ATF developed Project Gunrunner to focus ATF's investigative, intelligence, and training resources on the suppression of firearms smuggling/trafficking to Mexico. Similarly, CBP operations support U.S. efforts to combat arms smuggling/trafficking based on three pillars: analysis of firearms and weapons-related data, information sharing, and coordinated operations. CBP liaisons at the EPIC FETIU will compile and disseminate information and intelligence about crime-related guns and suspect guns, firearm thefts and losses, purchase patterns, suspicious purchasers, secondary gun markets, and other data related to firearms activity. **Action: ATF, CBP, ICE**

B. Deploy additional non-intrusive inspection equipment and canine teams in Mexico

Providing the Government of Mexico with non-intrusive inspection support and canine inspection team training at interior checkpoints will deny routes to traffickers in the most remote areas. CBP will take the lead on this initiative with its Mexican counterparts. **Action: DHS/CBP**

> **3. Enhance cooperation with international partners in weapons smuggling/trafficking investigations**

A. Engage in international training on border security, post-blast investigations, firearms identification, and detection of concealment traps used for smuggling/trafficking of firearms in vehicles

U.S. Government training programs can be expanded to more officials and include additional relevant curricula. Programs such as the Export Control and Related Border Security Assistance Program, the U.S. Government's premier initiative to help member countries improve their export control systems, would prove beneficial to Government of Mexico officials in their efforts to combat the flow of illegal weapons into and out of their country. Mexican and Central American authorities also may request training and associated equipment from DOD, if appropriate under existing programs and agreements. In addition, U.S. law enforcement will continue to host training opportunities in the United States for foreign officials, as well as provide investigative instruction at law enforcement academies in Mexico. **Action: DOJ/ATF, DOD, DHS/ICE**

B. Complete and enhance the deployment of Spanish eTrace capabilities among appropriate Mexican law enforcement agencies

Firearms tracing is the systematic tracking of a firearm from its manufacturer or importer through the chain of distribution, from wholesalers and retailers to the first retail purchaser. In October of 2010, the Government of Mexico signed an MOU with ATF to start comprehensive firearms tracing, and plans are underway to train over 200 PGR representatives by the end of 2011 in how to correctly utilize eTrace. ATF anticipates that upon conclusion of the Spanish eTrace deployment and training in Mexico in 2011, the Government of Mexico will be able to independently achieve comprehensive firearms tracing that would allow them to identify the methods, trends, trafficking patterns, routes and cells responsible for the illegal flow of weapons from the United States into Mexico. **Action: DOJ/ATF**

C. Continue to monitor the end-use of firearms legally exported from the United States to Mexico through the Department of State's Blue Lantern Program

The export of firearms from the United States is regulated by the Department of State's Directorate of Defense Trade Controls (DDTC) via the provision of DSP-5 export licenses. In order to verify that controlled commodities exported out of the United States are being used consistent with the authorization, the Department of State developed the "Blue Lantern" end-use monitoring program. Blue Lantern is a cooperative effort between DDTC, U.S. embassies or consulates overseas, and host governments to monitor the end-user and end-use of U.S. defense exports. DDTC will continue to target firearms transactions to Mexico for end-use monitoring, and ICE, in coordination with CBP's NTC-C, will work diligently to support State in identifying firearms shipments prior to export and increase the number of end-user verification checks. Primary support on this initiative will be provided by ICE agents assigned to attaché offices in Mexico. **Action: DOS, DHS/ICE**

D. Expand the deployment of ATF and ICE liaison officers in Mexico

The Mexico Border Liaison Officer (BLO) program allows ATF and ICE to identify and combat cross-border criminal organizations more effectively by providing a streamlined information and intelligence sharing mechanism between U.S. and Government of Mexico law enforcement personnel. In addition, the expansion, in coordination with the Government of Mexico, of permanent ATF and ICE investigators working in attaché offices throughout Mexico is critically important for facilitating cross-border coordination of weapons trafficking investigations. In 2011, ATF will expand its authorized positions in Mexico to include a high-level Country Attaché who will be placed at the U.S. Embassy in Mexico City. ICE currently has approximately 50 Border Liaison Officers situated along the Southwest border and ICE Attaché personnel in several locations in Mexico. **Action: DOJ/ATF, DHS/ICE**

E. Modernize, expand, and network ballistics imaging technology with Mexican law enforcement agencies

Integrated Ballistic Identification System (IBIS) equipment allows firearms technicians to acquire digital images of the markings made by a firearm on bullets and cartridge casings for use in comparing and matching ballistic evidence recovered at thousands of crime scenes, casing-by-casing and projectile-by-projectile. Ballistics information systems currently deployed in Mexico will begin linking in 2011 with a modernized National Integrated Ballistics Information Network (NIBIN) system to enable U.S. and Mexican law enforcement to discover links between crimes more quickly. **Action: DOJ/ATF**

4. Strengthen domestic coordination on weapons smuggling/trafficking investigations

A. Improve support to state and local law enforcement efforts targeting illegal weapons trafficking

ICE provides support to state and local law enforcement to target illegal weapons smuggling/trafficking through joint south-bound enforcement operations, its use of Title 19 cross-designation, and through joint operations with the BEST initiative. Additionally, ATF offers training to state and local law enforcement in such areas as firearms identification, firearms trafficking, explosives identification, and post-blast investigation. **Action: DOJ/ATF, DHS/ICE**

B. Increase ATF staffing levels in the Southwest border region

ATF is increasing the number of its Border Liaison Officers (BLO's) along the Southwest border. In addition, 7 new Project Gunrunner site cities have been identified and proposed. In early May 2011, 2 new ATF field offices will begin operating in Sierra Vista, AZ and Brownsville, TX, with the remaining 5 proposed offices to be opened as necessary funding becomes available. A total of 9 ATF offices are currently dedicated to Project Gunrunner. Project Gunrunner, ATF's initiative to counter weapons smuggling/trafficking, is a crucial part of the overall U.S. Government strategy to reduce the armed violence occurring in Mexico and the United States. **Action: DOJ/ATF**

C. Expand the use of the BESTs to disrupt cross-border weapons trafficking networks

BESTs are designed to leverage Federal, state, local, tribal, and foreign law enforcement and intelligence resources on the border in an effort to identify, disrupt, and dismantle criminal organizations such as those involved in weapons trafficking. The task forces are designed to increase information sharing, maximize investigative authorities, and promote collaboration among the participating agencies focusing on the identification, prioritization, and investigation of emerging or existing threats. **Action: DHS/ICE**

D. Continue applying standard proviso on export licenses requiring the provision of serial numbers for firearms exported to Mexico

By capturing the serial number of firearms when they are exported, U.S. authorities are able to provide foreign law enforcement with immediate and actionable intelligence, such as the date the weapon was exported and to whom the weapon was exported. This gives the foreign government a starting point in their country for an investigation. Capturing serial numbers at the time of export also allows the U. S. Government to rapidly identify if a weapon utilized in a foreign violent crime was smuggled out of the United States or if it was lawfully exported. The Department of State has instituted a policy to require and retain serial numbers on all United States Munitions List Category I, II, and IV firearms that have been granted authorization to be exported from the United States to Mexico. Provisos placed on these export license applications require applicants to upload serial numbers into the export licensing database prior to shipment. In addition, all such exports to Mexico are generally limited to government entities. **Action: DOS**

E. Improve United States Government outreach and coordination with Federal Firearms Licensees (FFLs)

Outreach to the firearms industry is a key component of ATF's firearms enforcement efforts. To this end, ATF investigates FFL applicants to determine eligibility and to educate them about their recordkeeping responsibilities, conducts compliance inspections of current FFLs, and collaborates with industry on voluntary compliance efforts. ATF Industry Operations Investigators conduct inspections of FFLs to detect diversion, ensure compliance with laws and regulations, and assist with business practices designed to improve compliance with the Gun Control Act. Additionally, ICE conducts industry outreach via Project Shield America in an effort to elicit cooperation from industry sources and provide information regarding U.S. export laws and potential threats from trafficking networks. As a result of these briefings, many potential violators are identified at the initial stages of their illicit activities. Continuing this coordinated outreach among U.S. agencies will lead to an increase in awareness and cooperation with the firearms industry. **Action: DOJ/ATF, DHS/ICE**

5. Increase successful Federal prosecutions for illegal weapons trafficking

A. Assign Violent Crime and Gang Unit prosecutors to the Southwest border

The Department of Justice's Gang Unit will continue to dedicate trial attorneys to work with various Southwest border intelligence centers, strike forces, Mexican law enforcement partners, and United States Attorneys' Offices to develop and prosecute gun smuggling/trafficking cases. Promoting and coordinating intelligence efforts can increase the ability of law enforcement officials to determine the involvement of drug trafficking organizations and gangs in gun smuggling/trafficking and associated violent crime along the border. **Action: DOJ**

B. Target Gun Trafficking Gangs

The ICE National Gang Unit oversees the following major operational and programmatic areas: Operation Community Shield; nationally coordinated ICE Specialized Urban Response Gang Enforcement (SURGE) operations; Racketeering Influenced Corrupt Organization investigations; Violent Crimes in Aid of Racketeering investigations; Continuing Criminal Enterprise investigations; and other criminal gang investigations. A large number of gang members are in the United States illegally. Moreover, many members of these criminal organizations have prior criminal convictions or are involved in crimes that have a nexus to the border, making them subject to ICE's broad scope of immigration and customs statutory and administrative enforcement authorities. ICE will continue to partner with Department of Justice's Violent Crime and Gang Unit prosecutors to develop a comprehensive and integrated approach to conducting complex criminal conspiracy investigations, short- and long-term gang SURGE enforcement operations, and other law enforcement efforts to address the threat posed by transnational street gangs. **Action: DHS/ICE**

C. Expand the Violent Crime Impact Team initiative to help address gang and violent crime issues along the Southwest border

ATF works to reduce violent crime by targeting and dismantling the gangs that pose the greatest threat to public safety. The Violent Crime Impact Team (VCIT) approach is one of many tools that ATF employs to address gang/violent crime violence. ATF's VCITs are integrated Federal, state, and local law enforcement initiatives focused on removing the most violent criminals and criminal organizations from the community. Southwest border VCITs are currently located in Houston and Laredo, Texas, and Tucson and Mesa, Arizona. ATF seeks to expand these initiatives at high need areas along the Southwest border to support its integrated strategy for the reduction of violent crime and the interdiction of illegal firearms. **Action: DOJ/ATF**

Chapter 8: Technology

Chapter 8 Strategic Objective

Provide improved technological capabilities and capacities for drug investigation and interdiction activities along the Southwest border

Background

The U.S. officers and agents who defend the Southwest border require state-of-the-art technology to counter the efforts of traffickers who have proven to be creative and adaptable in their attempts to evade law enforcement. The U.S. Government needs to commit resources to the on-going effort to research, develop, and deploy technologies that support the counternarcotics effort. The purpose of this chapter is to direct the development and fielding of emerging and state-of-the-art technologies to further Southwest border counternarcotics efforts as a part of broader efforts underway to improve operational control of the border. Technological enhancements in FY2011-2012 will help continue the development of the solutions initiated in FY 2010 to improve capacities in the following areas:

- Detecting, tracking, and classifying all threats along the land and maritime borders. Particular needs include technologies to support detection in rugged and subterranean environments, to include tunnels and semi-submersible detection. License plate recognition systems will be used to screen vehicular traffic.

- Wide-area surveillance for detection, identification, and tracking from the coast to beyond the horizon, including port and inland waterways. Particular needs include detection (and the capability to geo-reference the images) of vessels between the port region and beyond the horizon, especially small vessels and semi-submersibles.

- Non-intrusive inspection capabilities to detect narcotics, bulk currency, and illegal firearms in cargo and vehicles. These capabilities include the detection of intrusion or unauthorized access, particularly into containerized, palletized, parcel, or maritime and air cargo. Technology efforts will improve the detection capability for the south-bound transport of money, weapons, and illicit contraband.

- Tools and technologies (including innovative wireless technologies and applications) that will allow border security law enforcement officers to perform inspections of vehicles and vessels more efficiently, effectively, and safely.

Progress related to each specific technology is described in the supporting actions below. One area of research was satisfied after commercially available technologies were identified and found to be suitable to identify weapons being fired. The technology combines infrared sensors and high speed data analysis to detect, locate, and classify a broad range of weapon firings.

The interagency community will continue to synchronize its collective efforts to 1) conduct research and development to improve tunnel detection capabilities; 2) improve the collection and sharing of tunnel-related information and intelligence, both within the U.S. interagency community and between U.S. authorities and their Mexican counterparts; and 3) establish and execute joint initiatives with Mexico directed at ending the construction and use of tunnels under the Southwest border. As part of this Administration's overall border security policy, this Strategy also supports the collective interagency effort to end the construction and use of tunnels and subterranean passageways for the purpose of smuggling illegal drugs into the United States.

Supporting Actions

1. **Employ state-of-the-art detection technology to interdict drugs and other contraband**

A. Improve screening and examination through non-intrusive cargo container inspection and improve inspection of hidden or closed compartments
Technology is required to facilitate the detection or identification of contraband items, such as drugs, bulk currency, and illegal firearms, threat materials, or stowaways. This technology will improve penetration, resolution, throughput, contrast sensitivity, reliability, mobility, and interoperability and will integrate with a future Automated Target Recognition capability. DHS will pursue Conveyance Security Device technology to detect the unauthorized opening of cargo containers in transit. The DHS will work to develop and deploy tools that allow the non-intrusive inspection of hidden and closed contents. In particular, these tools should possess the ability to find contraband and security threats on vessels, in vehicles, and within cargo. **Action: DHS/CBP, DHS/S&T, DHS/ICE, DHS/USCG, DHS/TSA, DOJ/DEA, DOJ/FBI**

B. Explore potential improvements in bulk currency detection technology
Existing technology is only capable of detecting large quantities of bulk currency in clandestine environments. Advances in this technology will make it possible to detect smaller amounts of concealed currency in containers, automobiles, and parcels as well as on body-carriers. DHS S&T has initiated a characterization effort associated with bulk currency that will exploit unique signatures of the vapors and ink in paper currency. This research lays the basis for detection capability that will be developed in the future. Coordination with U.S. Secret Service, Treasury, and the ICE Bulk Cash Smuggling Center has benefited this research and operational constructs. Efforts in this area will continue, with DHS identifying the key components for the detection of bulk currency. **Action: DHS/S&T, Treasury, DHS/ICE, DHS/CBP, DOJ/DEA, ONDCP/CTAC**

C. Improve the capability to continuously track illegal transportation of contraband in vehicular traffic
LPR technology efforts are being utilized successfully on the Southwest border. The ONDCP Counterdrug Technology Assessment Center (CTAC) recently provided 94 dual stream cameras to support CBP and other agencies working with the HIDTAs on the Southwest border. **Action: DHS/S&T, ONDCP/CTAC, DHS/CBP, DOJ/DEA**

D. Improve the capability to continuously track illegal transportation of contraband on ships or containers

A particular need is the ability to conceal transponders while maintaining effective transmissions. This technology would help to link illegal shipments to the organizations that are smuggling those shipments. DHS S&T will explore options for addressing this challenge. **Action: DHS/S&T**

2. **Improve sensor, data fusion, and data sharing technologies**

A. Provide data fusion and automated tools for command center operations

These technologies will allow command centers to view entire scenes, provide alerts about anomalous and illegal activity, automate the ability to compare current tasking and location of blue forces to new events, recommend courses of action, and share information and collaborate with other non-collocated command centers. ONDCP/CTAC is working on an interagency agreement with DHS Office of Counternarcotics Enforcement on the development and implementation costs for a law enforcement cloud computing architecture which will provide highly automated, collaborative information-sharing capability across agencies conducting counter-illicit smuggling operations.

Eight sites representing interagency partners have been selected for Phase I of this project: EPIC, JTF-North, JIATF-S, Operation Bahamas and Turks-Caicos (OPBAT) Operation's Center, San Diego Law Enforcement Coordination Center (SD-LECC), U.S. Coast Guard Intelligence Coordination Center (USCG ICC), AMOC, and Customs and Border Protection Law Enforcement Technical Center (CBP LETC) Tucson. Following site surveys to assess the respective requisite infrastructure, analytic abilities, and operational requirements, as well as policies, sharing agreements, and legal considerations for each site, further research and development will be required to refine the software for initial database integration. EPIC will have the responsibility for integrating the data using the software architecture which is developed under this research funding and subsequently shared across the entire law enforcement community. **Action: DHS, DOJ, DOD, EPIC**

B. Increase information fusion, anomaly detection, and automatic target recognition capabilities for cargo

Enhanced technology is required to improve the capability to detect anomalous patterns in shipping data, cross-border vehicle data, and cross-border passenger data. Technology is also required to provide an automated imagery detection capability for anomalous cargo container contents such as stowaways, hidden compartments, and contraband. DHS continues to develop imagery technology associated with anomaly detection and reliable target recognition. **Action: DHS/CBP, DHS/S&T, DHS/ICE, DHS/USCG, DHS/TSA**

3. **Enhance communication and intelligence technologies**

A. Continue to establish classified SIPRNET via ADNET-S communication capabilities in the Southwest Border HIDTA Investigative Support Centers

This network will link the Southwest Border HIDTA Investigative Support Centers, supported by National Guard intelligence analysts, to EPIC and JTF North. The intelligence network will leverage military, law enforcement, and intelligence resources to provide greater interagency coordination, collaboration, and cooperation. The classified communication system will provide network members a secure means to disseminate up-to-date information. SIPRNET via ADNET-S communication capabilities for the Southwest Border HIDTA Investigative Centers have been completed in West Texas, New Mexico, and Arizona, and installation has begun at the Los Angeles Investigative Center as well. The remaining sites should be completed in FY 2011 if funding is available. **Action: DOD, ONDCP, DHS, ONDCP/Southwest Border HIDTA, EPIC**

B. Enhance development, coordination, and sharing of intelligence and information databases, communications systems, and tools

A wide range of intelligence-related databases and information systems have been established to facilitate the processing and sharing of intelligence information, both within the Federal community and with state and local partners. The Federal Government should examine existing structures and processes to identify ways to better integrate and consolidate their effectiveness and reduce instances of inadvertent duplication. Agencies collecting law enforcement seizure data on illegal drug, currency, and weapons removals on the Southwest border should electronically stream their data to EPIC for inclusion in the National Seizure System (NSS), the system for tracking all-agency illegal drug, currency, and weapons removals. In addition, new protocols should be developed for coordination among Federal and state agencies to enhance intelligence sharing as new fusion centers are established. **Action: DHS, DOJ, DOD, IC, ONDCP/HIDTA, DOJ/OCDETF, EPIC**

4. **Develop capabilities to detect, identify, track, and interdict small vessels, including self-propelled semi- and fully submersibles**

A. Improve and develop methods to conduct wide-area surveillance

Due to the continued effectiveness of U.S. and allied interdiction efforts in the transit zone, drug traffickers are attempting to use new and innovative methods to transport drugs to the United States, including the development and enhancement of low-profile and self-propelled semi- and fully submersible vessels. To counter these new methods, enhanced capabilities are required for wide-area surveillance to support the detection, identification, tracking, and interdiction of target vessels in the transit zone and in the maritime approaches to the United States.

Although other areas are subject to attempted exploitation by these submersibles and pleasure boats to clandestinely transport contraband, the target vessels most often encountered off the coast of San Diego, California and the Gulf of Mexico are 20- to 30-foot long fishing boats with outboard engines known as pangas (Pacific) and lanchas (Gulf). Intelligence gathered through the apprehension of these vessels has revealed they usually transit 30 or more miles north before turning sharply inland to offload their cargo. The interagency community will continue to seek technological solutions to these transit zone surveillance challenges. **Action: DHS/S&T, DHS/CBP, DHS/USCG, ICE, DHS/I&A, DHS/OPS, DHS/CNE, DOD, IC**

5. **Develop the capability to detect clandestine and infrastructure tunnels used for illegal activities**

A. Detect cross-border clandestine tunnels and activities occurring within existing tunnels

Cross-border tunnels are constructed and used to move people and contraband across the Southwest border at an alarming rate. Recently, tunnels have been detected that exhibit a higher degree of engineering and sophisticated construction techniques. These tunnels are deeper and longer than previously encountered and therefore, new methods are required to detect them. Additionally, the existing storm drain infrastructure on the Southwest border is being utilized to transport narcotics. Interagency efforts continue to develop technology to address these issues (see Appendix A for more details). **DHS/S&T**

Chapter 9: Strong Communities

Background

The consumption and production of illicit drugs along the U.S.-Mexico border erodes societies, endangers families, and provides illicit earnings that fuel corruption, crime, and violence. Illicit drugs and the drug culture lure children away from school, and adults away from legitimate work. On February 25, 2010, the Declaration of Drug Demand Reduction Cooperation was signed at the 8th U.S.-Mexico Bi-National Drug Demand Reduction Policy Meeting held in Washington, D.C. The declaration underscored the concept of co-responsibility and acknowledged the duty to take action domestically, bilaterally, and regionally to reduce drug use.

Drug-related crime and public safety challenges faced by these border communities include gang violence, home invasions, robberies, kidnappings, and the significant dangers associated with methamphetamine manufacturing. As the level of violence increases within a community, the fear of continued and escalating violence among community members may lead to a downward spiral, as individuals may be less likely to participate in community life. Fear of crime may also impact business conditions, as customers become unwilling to enter the community.

Evidence suggests that the most effective prevention strategies actively engage the communities they serve. Communities can be mobilized to identify, plan, direct resources, and undertake effective action for health promotion and health-enhancing social change. Various Federal, state, local, and tribal programs are underway to build stronger border communities. These initiatives should be expected to expand and coordinate their efforts to maximize outcomes. In addition, the Government of Mexico has quickly formed a network of governmental and non-governmental centers to prevent and treat drug abuse and addiction.

Due to the deep links between communities on both sides of the border, some prevention and treatment initiatives will necessarily include participants from Mexico as well as the United States. This not only strengthens resistance to drug use by participants, but also fosters stronger relationships between organizations, agencies, and individuals from both sides of the border.

Supporting Actions

1. **Develop strong, resilient communities on both sides of the border that resist criminal organizations and develop a culture of lawfulness**

A. Improve data collection and two-way information sharing between community members and police

Although substantial progress has been made in the nature and degree of drug-related data collected and shared along the border, further information, such as the relationship between violence and drug use, would be beneficial to share with community leaders to assist in decision making. HIDTAs will continue their efforts to identify and share relevant information with community-based coalitions. Similarly, community-based coalitions, such as those supported by the ONDCP-funded Drug Free Communities (DFC) program, often hold data that can help law enforcement respond more effectively to threats within their communities. The HIDTAs and other law enforcement entities will utilize local-level data to inform decisions to address the consequences associated with drug use in communities along the border. This should include the expansion of strategies utilized by the Department of Justice's Community Oriented Policing Services (COPS) that build relationships and encourage trust between local police and community members. **Action: ONDCP, DOJ**

> The Drug Free Communities support program created by the Drug Free Communities Act of 1997, is the Nation's leading effort to mobilize communities to prevent youth drug use. Directed by ONDCP, the DFC program provides grants to local drug-free community coalitions to increase collaboration among community partners and to prevent and reduce youth substance use. Recognizing the fundamental concept that local problems need local solutions, DFC-funded coalitions engage multiple sectors of the community and employ a variety of strategies to address local drug problems.

B. Enhance tribal, regional, local, and cross-border coalition efforts

A number of Federal, state, tribal, and local efforts are underway to strengthen community infrastructure. For example, the United States-Mexico Border Health Commission (BHC) was created as a binational health commission in July 2000 designed to provide international leadership to optimize health and quality of life along the U.S.-Mexico border. The BHC was created to serve all the people who reside within 100 kilometers, or 62 miles, on either side of this international boundary line. Specifically, this consists of six Mexican states and four states in the U.S., The Southwest Regional Substance Abuse Collaborative, developed and supported by the New Mexico Office of Border Health, facilitates a regional effort to prevent and decrease substance abuse and violence by linking resources to needs in a strategic and shared action plan across 10 counties in New Mexico as well as El Paso, Texas. These efforts should continue to be supported and their coordination with other initiatives already underway enhanced.

ONDCP will continue to strengthen community-based coalitions in several ways. The California Border Alliance Group Drug Demand Reduction (part of the Southwest border HIDTA) will continue to operate Forces United, which was developed in partnership with Californians for Drug Free Youth along with several local coalitions, the California Bureau of Narcotic Enforcement, California National Guard Counter Drug Task Force Drug Demand Reduction Team, the DEA, local sheriff offices, and local police departments. Efforts undertaken by this and other HIDTAs on the Southwest border will attend to such critical issues such as clandestine laboratory enforcement and drug endangered children. Through its "Above the Influence" initiative, ONDCP will offer additional resources for local youth-serving prevention groups to use with teens in their respective local communities. In addition, ONDCP will make available to communities additional anti-methamphetamine prevention resources, such as public service announcements (PSAs) capable of being customized, via www.methresources.gov. **Action: ONDCP, DOJ, HHS**

The National Anti-Drug Youth Campaign (Campaign) increases teen exposure to anti-drug messages through a combination of paid advertising (e.g., television, Internet, and cinema) and public communications (e.g., community events, corporate sponsorships with youth brands, and youth-centered activities). The Campaign has two distinct areas of focus: a teen-targeted Above the Influence campaign, and a young adult- targeted Anti-Meth campaign. In addition, the Campaign recognizes that it is at the community level where youth substance abuse prevention must ultimately occur. To this end, the Campaign will provide a model for delivering paid media, on-the-ground activities, local partnerships, Public Service Announcement materials, and news media attention to at-risk communities. On-the-ground activities and local partnerships will be key in allowing the Campaign to reach teens across multiple domains, including schools, clubs, worksites, faith communities, and recreational programs.

C. Strengthen Federal prevention efforts along the Southwest border

The Drug Free Communities program will provide grants to local drug-free community coalitions to increase collaboration among community partners and to prevent and reduce youth substance use. The Department of Justice will make available its PACT360 (Police and Communities Together) community prevention education program supported by DOJ's Office of Justice Programs in collaboration with the Partnership at drugfree.org. Latino360 brings PACT360 to the Hispanic community, with a presentation specifically tailored to reflect the unique needs of the Spanish-speaking community in the United States. The Southwest Regional Expert Team and the Western Regional Expert Team of SAMHSA's National Center for the Application of Prevention Technologies (CAPT) provide training and technical assistance, especially on the Strategic Prevention Framework with requests emanating from the four U.S. border states. In addition, HHS's Rural Assistance Center (RAC) will continue to act as a resource center for a range of available programs, funding, and research for providers serving rural residents, including those along the Southwest border. DEA will continue its annual promotion of Red Ribbon week, which reaches millions of Americans during the last week of October every year. By wearing red ribbons and participating in community anti-drug events, young people pledge to live a drug-free life. **Action: DOJ, HHS**

D. Enhance efforts to protect border communities from criminal threats

Border communities are exposed to unique drug-related stressors that impact the efforts of community-based prevention and treatment providers. Federal, state, local, and tribal law enforcement agencies have enhanced efforts to address these stressors through coordinated enforcement efforts with community-based providers. ICE will continue to coordinate with Federal, state, local, tribal, and foreign law enforcement counterparts through BESTs. Operation Stonegarden, a Federal Emergency Management Agency (FEMA) grant program, enhances security for communities along the border through increased patrol activities of state, local, and tribal law enforcement in areas that are vulnerable to criminal threats.

Moreover, the ICE initiative Operation Community Shield will continue to focus on coordinated enforcement actions that disrupt, dismantle, and prosecute criminal street gang members. In addition, CBP will continue to implement Operation Detour, a public awareness campaign to prevent youths from being lured by drug trafficking organizations to engage in specific criminal activity. **Action: DHS, DHS/ICE**

> Conceived by the U.S Customs and Border Protection in collaboration with local and state law enforcement agencies in Texas, "Operation Detour" is a public awareness campaign targeting high school students to prevent efforts by drug trafficking organizations to lure young adults into engaging in criminal activity. The campaign consists of an hour-long program that includes two videos explaining how the drug trafficking organizations are organized and what the consequences are for participating in these organizations. The presentation also includes a slideshow that explains the various criminal activities associated with drug smuggling. Also incorporated is a panel discussion with law enforcement officials explaining how their organizations enforce the law and what the potential penalties are for getting caught in narcotics trafficking.

2. **Continue development and implementation of evidence based and culturally appropriate prevention and treatment techniques and strategies**

A. Continue to research and disseminate evidence based prevention practices to border communities
With the support of the National Institutes of Health (NIH), significant progress has been made over the past decade in identifying effective interventions to prevent drug use among youth. Of the over 60 prevention interventions listed in SAMHSA's National Registry of Evidence Based Programs and Practices (www.nrepp.samhsa.gov), at least 25 include a focus on Hispanic youth in rural communities, and eight among tribal populations. NIH should continue to support research on prevention programs and their effectiveness for application with various border populations in reducing drug use and drug-related HIV acquisition. HHS will continue to disseminate these evidence-based findings through its training and technical assistance resources such as CAPT. The southwest and western sectors of the CAPT provide training on identifying and selecting evidence-based interventions, as well as offer training for prevention specialists. Several American Indian tribes, including the Tohono O'odham Nation, which traverses the border on both sides, have been eligible to participate in a Service to Science Academy which assists local programs, especially indigenous ones, to become eligible for developing evidence-based interventions. In addition, ONDCP's Southwest Border HIDTA will continue to partner with Federal, state, tribal, and local agencies and organizations on prevention initiatives. **Action: HHS, ONDCP**

B. Continue to research and disseminate evidence-based treatment practices to border communities
In spite of a number of evidence-based treatment interventions that have been tested with Hispanic and American Indian populations, few are available to address the unique treatment needs of youth in these populations. One exception is the Brief Strategic Family Therapy model that has been tested with substance-abusing Hispanic adolescents. This model is currently being tested for use in San Antonio, Texas, in a program targeted at substance abusing, gang-affiliated Mexican-American adolescents. NIH should continue to support research on effective culturally appropriate interventions and SAMHSA should continue to disseminate these findings. **Action: HHS**

> Brief Strategic Family Therapy is clinically-tested intervention designed to (1) prevent, reduce, and/or treat adolescent behavior problems such as drug use, conduct problems, delinquency, sexually risky behavior, aggressive/violent behavior, and association with anti-social peers; (2) improve pro-social behaviors such as school attendance and performance; and (3) improve family functioning, including effective parental leadership and management, positive parenting, and parental involvement with the child and his or her peers and school. The intervention was developed by University of Miami's Jose Szapocznik, Ph.D, and was tested for effectiveness with primarily Hispanic adolescents and their families.

3. Continue to integrate substance use disorder services into mainstream medicine

A. Collaborate with rural and community health centers along the border

Community health centers supported, in part, by HHS' Health Resources and Services Administration (HRSA) provide comprehensive, culturally competent, quality primary healthcare services to medically underserved communities and vulnerable populations. These include low income populations, the uninsured, those with limited English proficiency, migrant and seasonal farm workers, the homeless, and those living in public housing. Substance abuse services are provided by many of these health centers, such as Border Area Mental Health Services, the largest provider of behavioral health services in southwest New Mexico. HHS' Indian Health Service (IHS) makes comprehensive health care services available to Federally recognized tribes, including the approximately 25 Native American Nations along the U.S.-Mexico border. Direct health care services are administered through a nationwide system of 12 area offices and 161 IHS and tribally managed service units. ONDCP will continue to collaborate with HHS to integrate behavioral health care into primary care, particularly with the planned expansion of community health centers and proposed alcohol and substance abuse brief intervention in emergency departments of IHS. **Action: HHS, ONDCP**

4. Improve the quality of care available by ensuring providers are competent

A. Enhance professional education and training programs

For the past six years, the SAMHSA-funded Pacific Addiction Technology and Transfer Center (ATTC) has partnered with the HRSA-funded Pacific AIDS Education Training Center to conduct training in the California and Arizona border communities. Other partnering agencies have included the U.S. - Mexico Border Health Commission, Imperial County Public Health Department, California STD/HIV Prevention Training Center, San Diego Health Department, San Ysidro Health Center, and Southeastern Consortium of Community Health. In 2011, the Caribbean Basin ATTC, Hispanic Center of Excellence, and the CSAT Hispanic /Latino Stakeholder Group updated the U.S. Hispanic Street Gangs guide and developed a culturally and linguistically competent science-based trainer-of-trainers curriculum.

Funded by HHS's Substance Abuse and Mental Health Services Administration, ATTC provides nation-wide, multidisciplinary resource for professionals in the addictions treatment and recovery services field. Consisting of 14 regional centers, including the Caribbean and Hispanic ATTC, the network serves to raise awareness, build skills, and change practices of providers.

The Border Institute of Excellence, operated by Aliviane, Inc., will train substance abuse counselors and outreach specialists to help educate families to recognize early signals of potential substance abuse, and inform them about intervention techniques and other resources to seek additional help and treatment.

The Affordable Care Act creates a new Prevention and Public Health Fund designed to expand and sustain the necessary infrastructure to prevent disease, detect it early, and manage conditions before they become severe. This new initiative will increase the national investment in prevention and public health, improve health, and enhance health care quality. Specifically, the fund will support a variety of prevention activities including public health infrastructure development, behavioral health and primary care integration, and workforce development. **Action: HHS, DOS**

The Affordable Care Act created a new Prevention and Public Health Fund designed to expand and sustain the necessary infrastructure to prevent disease, detect it early, and manage conditions before they become severe. In FY2010, these new funds were dedicated to four critical priorities:

Community and Clinical Prevention: The initiative supports prevention activities that are known to reduce health care costs and improve the promotion of health and wellness, including the integration of primary and behavioral healthcare.

Public Health Infrastructure: The allocation strengthens state and local capacity to prepare health departments to meet 21st century challenges, including infrastructure development through improved information technology, workforce training, and regulation and policy development.

Research and Tracking: The initiative supports the Affordable Care Act's expansion of coverage for community and clinical preventive services by increasing resources for guidance and evaluation of preventive services.

Public Health Training: These funds support the training of existing and next generation public health professionals to advance preventive medicine, health promotion and disease prevention, and improve the access and quality of health services in medically underserved communities.

B. Expand training and certification of community health workers

Community Health Workers (promotores) are natural leaders within their communities and can act as liaisons to providers of health services and contribute to building the communities' capacity to respond to challenges and opportunities in a culturally congruent and competent manner. Several years ago, Texas instituted a certification program for promotores, with nearly 600 certified individuals reported as of May 2009. A study is currently underway by Texas Tech University Health Science Center on training promotores to conduct screenings and brief interventions in emergency department settings. Federal, state, and local efforts should continue to support developing this important component of the health care workforce. Findings from this study should be incorporated into planned and future border training initiatives and be incorporated into the HHS Office of Minority Health's action plan for reducing health disparities. **Action: HHS, DOS**

5. Interrupt the cycle of drug use, violence, and crime

A. Continue to support drug courts in border communities

By increasing direct supervision of offenders, coordinating public resources, and expediting case processing, drug courts can help break the cycle of criminal behavior, alcohol and drug use, and incarceration. A decade of research indicates drug courts reduce crime by lowering re-arrest and conviction rates, improve substance abuse treatment outcomes, reunite families, and produce measurable cost benefits. DOJ/OJP and HHS/SAMHSA will continue to support adult, juvenile, and family drug courts along the Southwest border. **Action: DOJ, HHS**

B. Provide reentry initiatives for offenders with substance abuse disorders returning to communities

Pivotal to creating an environment conducive to recovery for offenders is a process of re-entry that begins when offenders are first incarcerated and ends with the offender's successful community reintegration, evidenced by lack of recidivism. This process should provide the offender with appropriate evidence-based services—including addressing individual criminogenic behavior—based on a re-entry plan which relies on a risk/needs assessment and which reflects the risk of recidivism for that offender. For offenders with substance abuse disorders, access to evidence-based treatment services is essential. Access to other reintegration needs is also necessary, such as employment, education, housing, family reunification and parenting support, and other economic opportunities to sustain their recovery while under the supervision of well-trained probation officers. DOJ will continue efforts to support community engagement and supervision of substance-involved offenders. **Action: DOJ**

Chapter 10: Cooperation with Mexico

Chapter 10 Strategic Objective
Enhance U.S.—Mexico cooperation on joint counterdrug efforts

Background

The U.S.-Mexican bilateral relationship has never been stronger than today, and it continues to improve, based on strong, multi-layered institutional ties that persist and grow. The Merida Initiative, agreed to by the U.S. and Mexican Presidents in 2007 and launched in 2008, underscores the commitment of both governments to improve the lives of citizens in both countries, working across a broad range of issues and within the context of mutual trust and shared responsibility. Both governments seek to disrupt and dismantle the criminal networks that traffic drugs into the United States and illegal weapons and illicit revenues into Mexico in order to ensure the security and well-being of Mexicans and Americans alike. Stopping the flow of firearms and bulk cash into Mexico is an important component of the larger strategy to secure our borders from the criminal organizations that use those resources to traffic contraband and perpetrate violence.

At the March 23, 2010 meeting of the High Level Group, Secretaries Clinton and Espinosa endorsed a shared vision for a "Beyond Mérida" strategy (see box below), the goals of which are to:

1. disrupt and dismantle organized criminal organizations;

2. institutionalize reforms to sustain rule of law and respect for human rights;

3. create a 21st century border; and,

4. build strong and resilient communities.

Both Governments are now intensifying their efforts to support the creation of stronger democratic institutions in Mexico, especially within the justice sector. The United States and Mexico are expanding the focus beyond law enforcement to include facilitation of legitimate trade and travel and cooperation in building stronger communities along the border that are resistant to the corrupting influence of organized crime. Today there is greater emphasis in U.S. assistance on supporting Mexico's criminal justice reforms mandated by a 2008 constitutional amendment and its institution-building efforts across its justice sector. Within this context, the U.S. Government is moving away from large equipment transfers and into an engagement that reinforces progress already made by Mexico in institutionalizing its capacity to sustain the rule of law and respect for human rights, build strong institutions, promote full civil society participation, and transform the nature of our borders. The United States and Mexico are also cooperating to support Mexican efforts to assert governmental authority and otherwise enhance local effectiveness within specific major cities that are especially violent, as cartels challenge each other—and the government.

We are also increasing our collaboration on a range of prevention, treatment and criminal justice issues with Mexico. The Mérida Initiative supports drug treatment, education, counseling, job creation, and targeted media designed to reduce drug abuse along the Southwest border. These efforts will continue to expand. On February 25, 2010, the Declaration of Drug Demand Reduction Cooperation was signed at the 8th U.S. - Mexico Bi-National Drug Demand Reduction Policy meeting held in Washington, DC. The declaration underscored the concept of co-responsibility and acknowledged the duty to take action internally, bilaterally, and regionally to reduce drug use. As stated, "Consumption of illicit drugs erodes societies, endangers families, and provides illicit earnings that fuel corruption, crime, and violence. Illicit drugs and drug culture lure children away from school, and adults away from legitimate work."

The goals of the new "Beyond Mérida" strategy are: 1) Disrupt and Dismantle Organized Criminal Organizations; 2) Institutionalize Reforms to Sustain Rule of Law and Respect for Human Rights; 3) Create a 21st Century Border; and 4) Build Strong and Resilient Communities. Prior Mérida Initiative funding supported the purchase of aircraft, IT systems, police and forensics equipment, canines and handlers, and non-intrusive inspection equipment, as well as the provision of support to Mexican justice sector institutions to target the organized criminal groups, disrupt their activities, and build strong justice sector institutions. In the future, Mérida Initiative funding will be reoriented to emphasize support to and help in building stronger democratic institutions in Mexico, especially the police and justice sector, expanding the prior focus on interdiction of contraband to include facilitation of legitimate trade and travel, and cooperating in building stronger communities that are resistant to the corrupting influence of organized crime. Mérida assistance will reflect the increased emphasis on supporting Mexican-initiated rule of law reforms and institution-building efforts across its justice sector, through increased training, advice, smaller equipment purchases, and other capacity-building activities at the Federal, state, and local levels of Mexican Government.

Supporting Actions

1. **Expand upon ongoing bilateral efforts to stem the flow of drugs, money and weapons across our shared border**

There are numerous references elsewhere in the Strategy to ongoing bilateral cooperation, providing some sense of the depth and breadth of the liaison which occurs daily. The actions listed here are in addition to those listed in earlier chapters.

A. Deepen local cooperation

Cooperation in counternarcotics enforcement at the border state and city level already exists, but can be improved, offering additional means through which to coordinate actions attacking criminal activities along our common border. Many instances of cooperation at the local and state levels are conducted independent of U.S. Government involvement or initiative, responding to local problems with local solutions. The United States encourages and supports such local-to-local initiatives as appropriate. Future U.S. assistance increasingly will involve technical support delivered directly by U.S. law enforcement agencies (LEAs) to their Mexican peers, at the Federal, state, and local levels, in such areas as police professionalization and prison management reform. This will complement any changes approved by the Mexican Congress to restructure the local and state police forces. U.S. assistance also promotes such long-term efforts as fostering a "Culture of Lawfulness" which now forms part of the national elementary school curricula and is taught to police officers in the border states, contributing to the formation of a stable, equitable, and secure democracy in Mexico. **Action: DOS, DOJ, DHS, DOD, USAID**

B. Enhance capacity building and training initiatives to strengthen Mexican agencies and institutions
The future emphasis of U.S. Government assistance in the area of law enforcement will increasingly focus on training and other forms of institution building. Training will often be provided directly by U.S. LEA active-duty personnel, who will be able to share the best practices and standard operating procedures of their home agencies with their Mexican LEA peers. Training will involve diverse activities such as: technological solutions to basic interdiction problems, including remotely detecting smuggling tunnels or sensing south-bound trafficking in arms and bulk cash in ways that minimize the disruption to licit trade and travel; techniques for data mining; targeting inspections using non-intrusive inspection equipment and dog/handler teams more efficiently, to make these inspections more effective and less a disruption to licit traffic; internal controls and other anti-corruption mechanisms; human rights and community policing; and lessons learned on demand reduction.

Future U.S. assistance will increasingly go toward supporting Mexico's reform of its national justice system, through activities such as training for courts administrators, judges, prosecutors, police, and other actors in the system. It will expand on existing efforts to encourage the use of alternative dispute resolution as a means to increase public access to justice and reduce congestion in the court system. It will also help buttress the police forces below the Federal level, in parallel to Mexico's own restructuring of these forces nationwide. U.S. assistance will help expand the reach of such critical Mexican institutions as the National Institute of Criminal Sciences (INACIPE), which has been unable to respond positively to all the training requests received from Mexican state and federal offices to help them navigate the transition from the inquisitorial to the accusatorial system. **Action: DOS, DOJ, DHS, DOD, Treasury, USAID**

C. Expand on existing bilateral mechanisms and create new ones
The numerous bilateral cooperative mechanisms already in place that help advance this Strategy include:

- Intelligence and information sharing to improve targeting of border threats (drugs, cash, arms, trafficking in persons, etc.);

- Operational coordination along the Southwest border to leverage greater impact for interdiction efforts on both side of the border;

- Bilateral air cooperation to support each countries' air interdiction operations;

- Stationing U.S. LEA liaisons in Mexico to improve the immediacy of coordination with local and state LEAs;

- Judicial cooperation with Mexico to enhance the capabilities of Mexican prosecutors, courts, judges, and other actors and support the transition of Mexico's entire justice system towards accusatorial system;

- Support for Mexico's efforts to root out corruption that supports drug trafficking and related crimes; and

- Maritime operations centers' operating procedures for the coordination of maritime interdiction efforts

Both countries are committed to realizing the full potential of such mechanisms at all levels of government. The opening of the Bilateral Implementation Office in August 2010 in Mexico City is an exceptional expression of this cooperation, wherein officials of both governments are working daily, side-by-side, to implement the Mérida Initiative projects as expeditiously as possible. Other examples include such bilateral agreements as the Maritime Operations Letter of Intent signed in 2008 by the U.S. Coast Guard, USNORTHCOM, and Mexico's Navy and Secretariat for Communications and Transportation, which established the means to develop exercise and execute maritime security and safety standard operating procedures for coordinated bi-national maritime operations. The USCG meets with Mexican Navy representatives twice a year at the Multilateral Maritime Counter Drug Summit, which facilitates closer collaboration and integration in maritime operations and finds solutions to issues that impede effective implementation of existing bilateral arrangements. **Action: DOS, DOJ, DHS, DOD, Treasury**

Appendix A: Tunnel Strategy

Overview

The on-going existence and use of clandestine cross-border tunnels represent a unique and growing threat to homeland security. Countering this threat requires a unique and coordinated response, which is described in this Strategy.

Criminal organizations have demonstrated enduring and ever-evolving capabilities to creatively construct and use tunnels to gain access beyond the border to transport narcotics, people, and other contraband into the continental United States. As of March 22, 2011, there were 135 tunnels discovered by U.S. law enforcement agencies. There were an additional 20 tunnel attempts that were discovered prior to crossing the U.S. border. Of the completed tunnels, all originated in Mexico and exited in California, Arizona, or Texas, except for one tunnel on the northern border with Canada.

Smuggling organizations are quickly adapting and evolving in their use of subterranean smuggling routes. Until recently, it was thought to be impossible for smugglers to tunnel under the Rio Grande River in Texas. In June 2010, United States Border Patrol Agents in El Paso, Texas, discovered a tunnel dug just two feet under the river that stretched 130 feet. Over 200 pounds of marijuana was seized and one individual was arrested by BEST agents working within the BEST Tunnel Task Forces (TTF).

An example of the sophistication of some of these tunnels was the November 25, 2010, discovery of a 2,200-foot cross-border tunnel in San Diego, California by BEST TTF agents. The tunnel traveled nearly half a mile at a depth of 90 feet and included shoring, electricity, ventilation, and a rail system to assist in ferrying contraband. The entrance was concealed under a hydraulic steel door in the kitchen of a Tijuana, Mexico, residence. The tunnel exited into a warehouse near the Otay Mesa Port of Entry. It is estimated that this tunnel took more than a year to construct at a likely cost of $1 million dollars.

The marked increase in the number and sophistication of tunnels along the Southwest border over the last several years is likely a result of increased pressure by Federal, state, and local law enforcement authorities against narcotics traffickers. Continuing enhancements to border security and aggressive enforcement on established overland routes will likely lead Mexican drug trafficking organizations to further increase their tunnel construction as an alternative method to smuggle drugs into the United States.

Since 2009, the DHS-lead BESTs have enhanced their work with DOD to create a combined approach to training agents on all aspects of cross-border smuggling tunnels by using the knowledge and resources of each component agency. In addition, DHS has joined forces with DOD to counter the threat in a more coordinated effort.

The length, number, and sophistication of the tunnels, as well as the extensive time and labor that go into their construction, suggest that smugglers consider tunnels to be a useful investment despite the risk of discovery and interdiction. This Strategy lays out an interagency approach to end the construction and use of tunnels for smuggling illegal contraband into the United States.

Strategic Challenges

Currently, we do not possess tunnel detection technology that is effective for all possible border tunnel/subterranean passage scenarios. Detection of tunnels is made more difficult by variations in soil and other environmental conditions from region to region, as well as by variations in the methods, procedures, equipment, and materials that are used in their construction. A closer examination of discovered tunnels and subterranean passages will provide valuable information about the strengths and weaknesses of existing detection technologies and can assist in improving detection capabilities. More importantly, exploiting intelligence derived from an identified tunnel and facilitating investigations linked to tunnels can enhance a strategic approach to dismantle the network enabling tunnel construction.

Information sharing and coordination are critical elements to improving the effectiveness of tunnel intelligence, detection, investigations, and interdiction. Multiple stakeholders, to include Federal, state, and local entities, all have access to information, intelligence, and trend data related to tunnel activity. This information needs to be shared, analyzed, and disseminated along the front lines.

Strategic Approach

Successfully countering the construction and use of tunnels and subterranean passages focuses on two critical capabilities: intelligence collection and the sharing of information related to the planning, financing, construction, and use of tunnels; and detection of tunnel construction and smuggling activities.

Intelligence collection should focus on identifying and verifying suspicious activities near commercial and private structures adjacent to the border, especially in densely populated areas where legitimate activities can easily mask illicit trafficking activities. Investigations of border tunnels discovered near Otay Mesa, CA, for example, have revealed that when information such as warehouse ownership records, investment and physical construction activities, stated purposes of use, actual activities in the surrounding area, and other available information area are all compared, the result is the emergence of suspicious and/or illogical linkages that do not fit the normal profile for a legitimate business in that specific location. Identifying such suspicious activities and locations through improved intelligence and surveillance will improve the ability of law enforcement to detect and stop tunnel construction activities. Enhanced monitoring and detection of tunnel construction and smuggling activities requires improvements in sensor technologies so law enforcement personnel can detect unexplained voids; acoustic, gravitational, electronic, and/or seismic anomalies; and subtle changes in ground moisture and/or subsidence (sinking), which could confirm the presence of tunnel construction and related activities.

A number of U.S. Government entities are focusing on improving their collective efforts to detect, identify, and investigate tunnel construction activities, as well as the presence and use of tunnels and subterranean passages for the smuggling of contraband.

Interdiction of tunnel construction and prosecution requires coordinated interagency support. Cooperation between governmental agencies will improve interagency collaboration, either by discovering the tunnels prior to completion or when a completed tunnel is discovered, providing the right amount of evidence and witness statements needed for a successful prosecution.

Department of Defense (DOD)

The U.S. Northern Command (USNORTHCOM), its subordinate organization Joint Task Force-North (JTF-North), and the National Guard provide the primary vehicles through which DOD supports law enforcement counternarcotics efforts within the United States and in cooperation with the Government of Mexico. Such support includes a USNORTHCOM Counter-Tunnel Initiative, which is examining enhanced tunnel detection technology and capabilities in conjunction with the DHS, other DOD elements, and international partners. Other on-going DOD counternarcotics support activities that enhance this effort include: international drug smuggling detection and monitoring; international partner capacity building; communications; information sharing; training; reconnaissance; analytical support; technological development; and infrastructure programs.

Joint Capabilities Technology Demonstration

DHS and DOD are cosponsoring a "Tunnel Detection" Joint Capability Technology Demonstration (JCTD). USNORTHCOM is the proponent for this demonstration, and as the technologies mature, they will be fielded to DHS and DOD for field operation. DHS and DOD are also developing a Joint Tunnel Testing Range (JTTR). The JTTR will directly support tunnel detection system research, development, testing, and evaluation, including the planned JCTD as well as other tunnel technology research and development.

Interagency Tunnel Task Force

An effective model that improved law enforcement efforts against tunnel activity is the BEST TTF. These TTFs encourage collaboration between investigators and agents from several agencies, including ICE, CBP, DEA, FBI, and DOD, in order to unite efforts and resources to combat the transnational tunnel threat. The TTFs leverage their collective efforts to enhance cooperation with Mexico and include Mexican authorities as required to support criminal investigations. BEST serves as the local point of contact for coordination on tunnel-related investigations and intelligence of investigative value while CBP serves as the POC for remediation, and field testing of detection technology. The National BEST Unit (which includes CBP and JTF-N representation) is also coordinating remediation and field testing efforts from a regional and headquarters perspective. Many of the investigators are the subject matter experts in support of tunnel detection activity and technology development.

These task forces continue to provide feedback to DOD and DHS concerning efforts to evaluate technologies which could meet the operational requirements for a tunnel detection field capability. DOD's Counterterrorism Technical Support Office (CTTSO) is currently developing capabilities to detect, locate, monitor, and disrupt subterranean operations in semi-permissive and non-permissive environments to allow tactical forces to conduct operations and counter hostile and/or criminal networks. CTTSO heads the Counter-Tunnel Operations Working Group (CTOWG) and coordinates CTOWG requirements with other CTTSO programs.

CTTSO Counter-Tunnel Projects of Interest:

- **Portable Ground Penetrating Radar**—battery powered, man-portable, ruggedized system to detect subterranean structures (tunnels, bunkers, and caches) to a minimum depth of 15 feet, with antenna configuration to allow for operation by one person and be employable in any terrain

- **Improved Underground Communications**—planned proof of concept to investigate if further funding is warranted; have looked at multiple available systems in technology demonstrations

- **Remote Imaging and Detection of Underground Anomalies**—proven prototype that implements laser technology to identify buried objects (e.g., caches, IEDs); will expand the development in FY 2011 to determine if technology is capable of detecting voids

- **Seismic-Acoustic Sensor Kit**—mobile seismic acoustic sensor system designed to detect underground activity with the intent of easy deployment and operation in a temporary environment (though permanent installation is also an option)

- **Canine Training Facility**—working to build a specialized canine training facility to develop training protocols for tunnel detection that can be implemented community-wide

- **Ongoing Data Exchange with the Israeli Ministry of Defense**—to share information, tactics, techniques and procedures (TTPs), and experiences

- **Development of a Counter-Tunnel Training Program** for DHS and its component agencies

The purpose of the CTOWG is to perform the following roles:

- Identify and discuss current and future threats/trends at home and abroad

- Present current technology development efforts:
  - Facilitate collaboration and consolidation of on-going parallel and complementary efforts
  - Act as the clearinghouse of technology solutions

- Identify user capability gaps and define interagency requirements to fill these gaps:
  - Locate current solutions or fund development of solutions
  - Merge capabilities to address both law enforcement and military requirements
  - Share identified technologies and capability gaps with appropriate subgroups within CTTSO

Department of Homeland Security (DHS)

Customs and Border Protection (CBP)

CBP is tasked with border security and is responsible for securing nearly 7,000 miles of land border. As CBP enhances security on the surface, in the air and in our maritime environment, criminals attempt to utilize illicit and non-illicit tunnels to smuggle their contraband, currency and weapons across our borders. Since the first documented illicit tunnel in 1990, 155 tunnels and tunnel attempts have been discovered by diligent law enforcement work, human intelligence, and in some case by accident. These tunnels have increased both in sophistication and construct causing a potential threat to national security.

In an effort to counter this threat, CBP has ongoing efforts to acquire and procure tunnel detection technology. Through market research and extensive studies by academia, CBP has identified viable technology solutions to detect tunnel construction activity prior to its completion. CBP is working towards creating an official program of record that when formalized will support the acquisition and deployment of tunnel detection technology.

CBP and HSI have partnered with the Department of Defense and other DOD entities, to test and evaluate tunnel detection technology designed by DOD's Army Core of Engineers and private industry.

Directorate of Science and Technology (DHS/S&T)

DHS/S&T is working with CBP, ICE, DOD, industry, and academia to identify, develop, test, and implement tunnel detection technologies. DHS/S&T's mission is to create high-risk/high-reward homeland security research and development projects that could lead to significant technology breakthroughs that would greatly enhance DHS operations.

In FY2010, DHS/S&T's Borders and Maritime Security Division (BMD) coordinated closely with CBP, ICE, DOD, and academia to conduct and coordinate research related to tunnel detection. Specifically, this research is aimed at identifying capability gaps and technologies that can be modified or further developed to achieve tunnel detection mission success. BMD will conduct a series of interviews, site visits, and workshops with CBP and ICE agents to identify and prioritize tunnel detection capability gaps. From these activities, DHS/S&T will be able to develop or enhance technologies that detect illegal tunnel activities. In addition, BMD will collaborate with CBP, ICE, DOD, and other strategic partners to develop a baseline understanding of international tunnel detection capabilities, best practices, and technologies being explored or employed. Results from this research may identify high-priority or emerging areas where S&T can invest additional R&D funds to make high-reward advances in tunnel detection.

In FY 2011, DHS/S&T will continue support and co-sponsorship of the Rapid Reaction Tunnel Detection (R2TD) Joint Capability Technology Demonstration (JCTD) with USNORTHCOM. This JCTD will provide a baseline system-of-systems technology suite for the detection, localization, and remediation of cross-border tunnels. Initial demonstration and testing of associated technologies in an operational environment began in May 2010 and is projected to continue through FY 2012. The Joint Tunnel Testing Range (JTTR) being constructed at Yuma Proving Grounds directly supports tunnel detection system research, development, testing, and evaluation, including the R2TD JCTD.

DHS/S&T continues to pursue innovative technologies that address high-interest areas where limitations in the baseline capability provided by the R2TD JCTD may exist. In FY 2009, an operationally relevant proof-of-concept demonstration was conducted for an advanced ground penetrating radar technology that showed potential to address operational needs in a projected baseline limitation area. Results warranted continued development efforts in FY 2010, with a depth performance verification test planned for FY 2011.

U.S. Immigration and Customs Enforcement (ICE)

ICE Homeland Security Investigations (HSI) serves as the lead agency for counter-tunnel investigations. The Border Tunnel Prevention Act, signed into law in October 2006, authorizes HSI with primary jurisdictional authority to investigate individuals and criminal organizations engaged in unlawful tunnel-related activities along the Southwest border. Currently, ICE HSI has five field offices actively engaged in counter-tunnel investigations: San Diego, CA; Calexico, CA; Yuma, AZ; Nogales, AZ; and El Paso, TX. ICE additionally integrates support from other relevant headquarters and field-based investigative and intelligence assets to support these efforts.

HSI field offices engage in counter-tunnel investigations primarily through the BEST TTF construct. A recent success resulted in the first prosecution under the 2006 Border Tunnel Prevention Act:

- On December 11, 2009, Mexican Military notified the HSI Calexico office of a partially built subterranean tunnel. The Mexican Office of the Attorney General (PGR) reported that individuals detained provided information that the exit point was in a warehouse in Calexico, California.

- On December 14, 2009, HSI special agents executed a search warrant at a warehouse located in Calexico, California, where they discovered the exit point to the tunnel. During the search of the tunnel, HSI special agents discovered a receipt from a hotel in El Centro, California, in the name of Daniel Alvarez.

- On December 21, 2009, Calexico HSI special agents arrested Alvarez for violating 21 U.S.C § 952, 960, and 963, conspiracy to import 5 kilograms or more of cocaine, and/or 1.5 kilograms or more of a mixture containing a detectable amount of methamphetamine. Alvarez entered a guilty plea to 18 U.S.C § 555, knowingly constructing a tunnel/passage into the United States and was sentenced in the Southern District of California to 15 months in Bureau of Prisons custody and three years of supervised release. This is the first time anyone has been convicted under this new law.

Tunnel Task Force (TTF) and the Border Enforcement Security Task Force (BEST)

In 2006, ICE HSI established the first TTF, which falls under the auspice of the BEST. In order to enhance Federal, state, and local de-confliction and coordination, counter-tunnel operations are coordinated locally through the San Diego, Calexico, Yuma, Nogales, Tucson, and El Paso BEST units. The BEST serves as the local point of contact for counter-tunnel investigations and intelligence while CBP serves as the POC for tunnel remediation, technology detection development, equipment field testing, state and local coordination, coordination with the United States Attorney's office, Congressional inquiries, rescue and emergency services, and community outreach. The TTF brings together investigators from several agencies including ICE HSI, CBP, FBI, DEA, DOD, and various state and local agencies to combat the tunnel threat.

On November 3, 2010, San Diego BEST TTF agents discovered a sophisticated 600-yard underground cross-border passageway that led to the seizure of 30 tons of marijuana, the 2nd largest drug seizure on U.S. soil with a value of approximately $30 million. The investigation started when TTF agents patrolling near the Otay Mesa Port of Entry followed a tractor trailer that was acting suspiciously. The truck was stopped at a U S. Border Patrol checkpoint in Temecula where agents found approximately 10 tons of marijuana. Following the seizure, BEST TTF agents searched the building the truck departed and discovered a 16-ton cache of marijuana and the entrance to the cross-border tunnel. Task Force agents quickly alerted Mexican military personnel who located the tunnel's other entrance at a warehouse in Tijuana. Inside that building, Mexican authorities recovered another four tons of marijuana.

ICE Cooperation with Mexico

ICE Assistant Attaché Tijuana is creating a joint ICE-Government of Mexico investigative tunnel response team that will focus on the identification and investigation of tunnels on the Mexican side of the border. The team will initially focus its efforts in the Tijuana area, eventually expanding its scope to respond to tunnels detected along the entire Southwest border.

ICE is currently in the process of purchasing emergency rescue and tunnel safety equipment for the Mexican military and SSP. In addition, ICE anticipates purchasing tunnel exploring robots in order to test the safety and stability of tunnels prior to entry by law enforcement. The ICE Assistant Attaché Tijuana, in coordination with the San Diego BEST TTF, will provide training to Mexican military and SSP officers on the proper use of ICE-provided equipment.

Criminal Penalties

The Border Tunnel Prevention Act, signed into law in October 2006, provides increased criminal penalties for persons who construct or use a tunnel or subterranean passageway for illegal purposes. This legislation amended Chapter 27 of Title 18, United States Code, to prohibit unauthorized construction, financing, or recklessly permitting the construction or use of a tunnel or subterranean passageway between the United States and another country on one's land. The specific provisions include:

- A 10-year prison term for any individual who recklessly permits the construction or use of a tunnel or subterranean passageway on land which is controlled by that individual

- A 20-year prison term for any individual who knowingly constructs or finances the construction of a tunnel or subterranean passageway that crosses the international border between the United States and another country, other than a lawfully-authorized tunnel or passage known to the Secretary of Homeland Security and subject to inspection by ICE

- A doubling of penalties for individuals who use a tunnel or subterranean passageway to unlawfully smuggle an alien, any controlled substance, weapons of mass destruction (including biological weapons), or any member of a terrorist organization

- Authorization for the forfeiture of any property involved in, or traceable to, the construction or financing of an illegal tunnel or subterranean passageway

Recommendations

- The Departments of Justice and Homeland Security should examine the efficacy of formally designating a violation of The Border Tunnel Prevention Act as a predicate offense for conducting a Title III wire intercept, recommending to Congress the addition of The Border Tunnel Prevention Act as a Specified Unlawful Activity for violations of the Money Laundering Control Act and creating provisions in the law for civil and criminal forfeiture

- DHS and DOD work together to develop a web-based information sharing tunnel forum that is paralleled on the unclassified, the secret, and the top secret levels. This would facilitate the sharing of information in all three forums in a centralized fashion.

Conclusion

As part of the Administration's overall border security policy, this Strategy supports the collective interagency effort to end the construction and use of tunnels and subterranean passageways for the purpose of smuggling illegal drugs into the United States. Terrorists have the potential to use already-established smuggling pathways—such as tunnels—to move contraband, personnel, and money across borders. It is essential that tunnels be viewed as a unique and growing threat to homeland security.

The interagency community will continue to synchronize its collective efforts to accomplish the following:

- Conduct research and development that leads to better tunnel detection capabilities;

- Continue to develop confidential sources to assist in tunnel detection;

- Improve the collection and sharing of tunnel-related information and intelligence, both within the U.S. interagency community and between U.S. authorities and their Mexican counterparts; and

- Establish and execute joint initiatives with Mexico directed at ending the construction and use of tunnels under the Southwest border.

The combination of strengthened criminal penalties, enhanced support for tunnel-related investigations, improved detection capabilities, and enhanced sharing of information will help to achieve these goals.

Appendix B: Resources

Overview of Funding for the National Southwest Border Counternarcotics Strategy		
	FY2010 Enacted	FY2012 Request
Intelligence and Information Sharing Efforts		
DHS/Immigration and Customs Enforcement	6,906	7,225
Subtotal, Intelligence and Sharing	*6,906*	*7,225*
Efforts at and between the Ports of Entry		
DoD/Drug Interdiction and Counterdrug Activities	55,798	41,783
DHS/Customs and Border Protection	763,140	798,845
Subtotal, Ports of Entry	*818,938*	*840,628*
Efforts against Air and Marine threats		
DoD/ Drug Interdiction and Counterdrug Activities	45,628	45,331
DHS/Customs and Border Protection	315,581	293,527
Subtotal, Air and Marine	*361,209*	*338,858*
Investigations and Prosecutions		
DHS/Immigration and Customs Enforcement	159,262	166,346
DoJ/Drug Enforcement Administration	373,061	408,343
DoJ/Office of Federal Detention Trustee	151,500	165,464
DoJ/Organized Crime Drug Enforcement Task Force	156,380	146,483
DoJ/U.S. Marshals Service	42,419	44,122
Subtotal, Investigations and Prosecutions	*882,622*	*930,758*
Cooperation with Mexico		
DoD/Drug Interdiction and Counterdrug Activities	74,929	58,735
DHS/Immigration and Customs Enforcement	1,465	2,060
DoS[2]/INCLE/ ESF	293,000	281,760
Subtotal, Cooperation with Mexico	*369,394*	*342,555*

---

2. Since both the Central America Regional Security Initiative and the Caribbean Basin Security Initiative are not included in the 2011 *Southwest Border Counternarcotics Strategy*, the Resource Annex doesn't capture the funding information of those initiatives.

Department of Defense

Program: National Guard State Plans

Resource Information:

	FY2010 Enacted (000)	FY2012 President's Budget (000)	Delta (FY2012 over FY 2010) (000)
Base Resources	55,114	41,201	(13,913)
Incremental Increase/ Decrease	-	-	-
Program Total	**55,114**	**41,201**	**(13,913)**

Program Description:

Resource information above only pertains to the four Southwest Border States (California, Nevada, Arizona, and New Mexico). The National Guard State Plans program supports only those missions which are Department of Defense (DoD) approved as militarily unique. The National Guard State Plans provide Air and Army National Guard counternarcotics support to federal, state, and local law enforcement agencies and community demand reduction organizations requesting assistance. The program is currently divided into six mission categories: (1) Program Management provides for the coordination, liaison, management of the program; (2) Technical Support provides linguist or translator support, intelligence analysis, investigative case support, communications support, engineer support, and subsurface diver support; (3) General Support includes eradication operations support; (4) Counternarcotics-related training provides training for law enforcement agencies and military personnel; (5) Reconnaissance/ Observation provides surface and aerial support. Surface support includes unattended sensor support, listening posts and observation posts using military equipment and ground surveillance radar. Aerial support is performed using both helicopters and fixed-wing aircraft as well as use of unmanned aerial vehicles; (6) Demand Reduction support includes various types of community based activities in which National Guard volunteers assist community groups in providing drug prevention information and education primarily to young children.

Department of Defense

Program: Joint Task Force—North

Resource Information:

	FY2010 Enacted (000)	FY2012 President's Budget (000)	Delta (FY2012 over FY 2010) (000)
Base Resources	11,337	9,692	(1,645)
Incremental Increase/ Decrease	-	-	-
Program Total	**11,337**	**9,692**	**(1,645)**

Program Description:

DoD established Joint Task Force-North (JTF-N) in 1989 to provide support to US counterdrug law enforcement agencies with militarily unique skills in areas such as operations, training, and intelligence in order to assist these agencies reduce the flow of drugs into the arrival zone. The primary focus of JTF-N is on designated High Intensity Drug Trafficking Areas (HIDTAs) and multi-agency DLEA requests. Funding for volunteer units supporting missions include travel costs, deployments and redeployments of units, expendable supplies, and contracted services. While supporting the missions of other agencies, DoD enhances its own military readiness.

Department of Defense

Program: Tethered Aerostat Radar System

Resource Information:

	FY2010 Enacted (000)	FY2012 President's Budget (000)	Delta (FY2012 over FY 2010) (000)
Base Resources	34,068	35,297	1,229
Incremental Increase/ Decrease	-	-	-
Program Total	**34,068**	**35,297**	**1,229**

Program Description:

The Tethered Aerostat Radar System (TARS) provides dedicated radar surveillance of the US Southwest Border, Florida Straits and Puerto Rico. The TARS present US Northern Command (USNORTHCOM) with a persistent, low-altitude small target surveillance capability that is critical for the detection and monitoring of aircraft meeting narcotics and narcoterrorism trafficking profiles at six sites along the U.S. southwest border (Yuma and Ft Huachuca, AZ; Deming, NM; Marfa, Eagle Pass, and Rio Grande, TX), as well as a seventh site at Cudjoe Key, FL, and an eighth site at Lajas, PR. Other users of TARS data include the North American Aerospace Defense Command (NORAD), the US Southern Command, the Department of Homeland Security (DHS), and Customs and Border Protection (CBP). The program funds approximately 233 contract employees spanning the eight sites, the Contract Management Office, the TARS Control Center, Engineering and Technical Services, and a Logistics Center. In addition, the program funds life cycle management, system enhancement, facility improvements, and government program management activities.

Department of Defense

Program: DOD Air and Marine Operations Center Support

Resource Information:

	FY2010 Enacted (000)	FY2012 President's Budget (000)	Delta (FY2012 over FY 2010) (000)
Base Resources	907	924	17
Incremental Increase/ Decrease	-	-	-
Program Total	**907**	**924**	**17**

Program Description:

The Department of Defense's (DoD) Air and Marine Operations Center (AMOC) Support provides Air National Guard (ANG) radar surveillance operators to support the AMOC. Operators provide radar surveillance, air track monitoring, and air track data recording and forwarding for identification of air tracks suspected of smuggling drug contraband across U.S. borders. The seven ANG personnel perform liaison duties and operate radar display consoles. Personnel coordinate enforcement activity with participating law enforcement agency (LEA) entities, USNORTHCOM, NORAD, and U.S. Air Force Air Defense Sectors. Personnel provide direct support to the AMOC, which includes intelligence analysis, communications sustainment, airspace surveillance/flight advisories, planning and implementation of special missions, Battle Staff Support, and expertise in DoD Air Defense and data link operations.

Department of Defense

Program: USNORTHCOM Mexico Counternarcotics Operational Support

Resource Information:

	FY2010 Enacted (000)	FY2012 President's Budget (000)	Delta (FY2012 over FY 2010) (000)
Base Resources	38,230	50,915	12,685
Incremental Increase/ Decrease	-	-	-
Program Total	**38,230**	**50,915**	**12,685**

Program Description:

USNORTHCOM Mexico CN Operational Support maintains, repairs, or upgrades existing equipment; trains security forces personnel; provides transportation, intelligence analysis, command and control, aerial reconnaissance, and the establishment of bases of operations or training facilities. CN training, taking place both inside and outside of the Continental United States, is directed at sustaining operational capabilities.

Department of Defense

Program: USNORTHCOM Enhanced Section 1033 Support

Resource Information:

	FY2010 Enacted (000)	FY2012 President's Budget (000)	Delta (FY2012 over FY 2010) (000)
Base Resources	5,720	7,820	2,100
Incremental Increase/ Decrease	30,979	-	(30,979)
Program Total	**36,699**	**7,820**	**(28,879)**

Program Description:

USNORTHCOM Enhanced Section 1033 Support includes the transfer of non-lethal protective and utility personnel equipment, the transfer and repair of non-lethal specialized equipment (including communications, photographic, radar, night vision), and the maintenance and repair of equipment for Mexico. The program increase in FY 2010 was a one-time, Congressionally directed spending item in the DoD Appropriations Act for FY 2010, which provided secure radios for Ciudad Juarez police units, a network of microwave-based communications system for 10 Mexico border cities, and secure tactical radios for Mexican military special forces units.

Department of Homeland Security, Customs and Border Protection

Program: Office of Border Patrol

Resource Information:

	FY2010 Enacted (000)	FY2012 President's Budget (000)	Delta (FY2012 over FY 2010) (000)
Base Resources	457,766	460,794	3,028
Incremental Increase/ Decrease	3,589	-	(3,589)
Program Total	**461,355**	**460,794**	**(561)**

Program Description:

The Office of Border Patrol (OBP) incorporates technology, infrastructure, personnel, and intelligence capabilities as critical elements of effective border interdiction efforts. Utilizing the proper mix of these elements is essential to the U.S. Border Patrol's operations to detect, identify, classify, and respond to all illegal cross border activities. A multi-layered defense provides the best enforcement posture for detecting and seizing illegal drugs. This multi-layered defense includes enhancements to U.S. Border Patrol checkpoints, the expansion of canine capabilities, the use of non-intrusive inspection (NII) equipment, and the leveraging of other resources that improve detection capabilities near checkpoints. Additional agents and resources, which are dedicated to detection and interdiction activities at and around checkpoints, have made a positive impact on counternarcotics efforts in the Southwest border (SWB) region.

The Border Patrol establishes and maintains effective partnerships, formal and informal, with state and local law enforcement agencies, as well as other federal agencies that have an interest in the border regions. OBP has increased the presence of Border Patrol agents assigned to U.S. Immigration and Customs Enforcement's (ICE) Border Enforcement Security Task Forces (BESTs) to address border crime and its associated violence. OBP also works closely with the HIDTA task forces to continue to improve collaborative enforcement efforts. Through FEMA's Operation Stonegarden, OBP utilizes grants awarded to state, local, and tribal agencies to enhance border security by funding an increased law enforcement presence in areas along the border.

Further, the Border Patrol maintains international partnerships, primarily with agencies of the Governments of Mexico and Canada, to enhance border security. In coordination with DHS, CBP has engaged Mexico, Central America, the Dominican Republic, and Haiti on the Merida Initiative in an effort to reduce drug demand, stop the flow of weapons moving south, and confront gangs and cross-border organizations. The Border Patrol International Liaison Unit (ILU) creates and maintains positive working relationships to foster alliances with foreign counterparts in order to increase border security. The alliances are established to foster and maintain open communications and mutual respect with and between foreign and domestic law enforcement counterparts.

In September 2009, the Border Patrol initiated ACTT as the next stage of border operations along the Arizona border. ACTT utilizes a collaborative, cooperative enforcement approach that leverages the capabilities and resources of the DHS agencies in partnership with other federal agencies, and state, local, and tribal governments. The purpose of this initiative is to achieve increased levels of border security, create a secure and safe border environment, reduce crime rate in affected communities, and improve quality of life for residents in the border areas. ACTT operations have targeted the Arizona/Sonora border area with the objective to deny criminal organizations from operating along approximately 80 miles of the Arizona border.

The Border Patrol also makes use of Forward Operating Bases (FOBs) for coverage of remote crossing points that have historically been very difficult for agents to patrol due to the vast distances and the time involved to access these areas. FOBs have proven to be very beneficial to the detection and deterrence of illegal entries in the areas in which they have been deployed. There are approximately 14 FOBs currently operating along the border and they will continue to be utilized in areas where the Border Patrol has a need to extend its reach. As the Border Patrol continues to gain operational control of the border, illegal migration activities and smuggler tactics shift in an attempt to identify and exploit vulnerabilities in border security measures, particularly in the more remote areas of the border. Strategically placed FOBs afford a distinct advantage in that they provide a cost effective, secure staging facility that allows agents to be forward deployed in close proximity to the border—thereby improving Border Patrol's capability to rapidly respond to and counter these shifts in illicit cross-border traffic.

Traffic checkpoints are critical components of the Border Patrol's enforcement-in-depth border security strategy and contribute significantly to gaining effective control of the Nation's borders. There are currently 34 permanent traffic checkpoints along the border. This strategy was developed to maximize resources and to increase the certainty of arrest of anyone posing a threat to the United States. Border Patrol checkpoints are strategically located on routes of egress leading away from the border, thus, greatly increasing the Border Patrol's detection and interdiction capabilities. A complete border security model that includes enforcement-in-depth creates an environment that denies, degrades and disrupts the criminal elements ability to exploit the infrastructure needed to conduct operations.

Department of Homeland Security, Customs and Border Protection

Program: Office of Field Operations

Resource Information:

	FY2010 Enacted (000)	FY2012 President's Budget (000)	Delta (FY2012 over FY 2010) (000)
Base Resources	164,076	250,830	86,754
Incremental Increase/ Decrease	4,888	8,929	4,041
Program Total	**168,964**	**259,759**	**90,795**

Program Description:

Inbound Activities

CBP's priorities on the SWB are to sustain gains made in the San Diego and Tucson corridors, and move the best practices of those efforts to the El Paso and Laredo corridors. CBP continues to run coordinated inbound and outbound enforcement operations along the SWB. These operations include participation by the OBP, ICE and state/local law enforcement agencies. These operations have proven to be successful in interdicting narcotics and outbound currency.

The Office of Field Operations (OFO) coordinated its efforts with OBP, ICE, DOJ and a host of state and local strategic partners in the establishment of the Alliance to Combat Transnational Threats (ACTT) in El Paso. A Unified Command structure has been established. ACTT planning and operation cells have coordinated a variety of operations to enhance intelligence collection and increase the number of investigations targeting transnational criminal organizations.

OFO is currently deploying additional CBP officers to the Tucson Ports of Entry and is identifying CBP Officers that would be available for future deployments at the El Paso Ports of Entry to further enhance the current enforcement efforts and allow for in increased tempo of operations.

Outbound Activities

On March 12, 2009, OFO re-established the Outbound Program Office in response to the on-going issues pertaining to violence and firearms smuggling on the SWB. CBP's outbound efforts are to ensure that there are trained CBP officers able to conduct outbound operations through adequate outbound facilities, equipment, and technology while working with international and other government law enforcement agencies. CBP employs a "pulse and surge[3]" strategy for outbound operations at most

---

3. "Pulse and surge" operations are short duration but periodic outbound inspections that are followed by periods without inspections. The operations are conducted either randomly and/or are intelligence driven. During "pulse and surge" operations, individuals and conveyances are stopped and a brief interview may take place. If further checks are required, the person or vehicle will be referred to "secondary" where further questioning and/or inspections occur. If during a secondary inspection Customs and Border Protection officers (CBPOs) encounter violations, they may make seizures, issue penalties, effect detentions, or make arrests depending on the seriousness of the offense. The very nature of "pulse and surge" operations allows for an immediate stand-down of outbound inspections in order to manage the traffic flow departing the port of entry.

SWB crossings. This allows for immediate stand-down of outbound inspections to manage traffic flow departing the port of entry. Additionally, CBP officers have been temporarily detailed over a period of time to support the Alliance to Combat Transnational Threats (ACTT) operations. The deployment of additional CBP officers to high priority ports supporting ACTT permits CBP to conduct 24/7 outbound operations to mitigate the threat posed by violent criminal enterprises working in these area.

CBP currently has 18 permanently assigned currency/firearm detector dog teams deployed to SWB ports of entry and plans to deploy an additional 14 teams in FY 2011. As of March 15, 2011, CBP has a total of 147 large-scale imaging systems deployed to and in between Ports of Entry (POEs) on the Southwest border, including 106 systems deployed to OFO POEs and 41 systems deployed to Border Patrol checkpoints. CBP has a total of 75 low energy NII imaging systems deployed to and in between POEs along the SWB, including 36 systems deployed to OFO POEs and 39 systems deployed to Border Patrol checkpoints.

Building on the initial success of the Western Hemisphere Travel Initiative (WHTI), CBP is optimizing inbound operations and leveraging license plate reader technologies and process improvements for outbound and checkpoint environments. During FY 2011, CBP will deploy outbound license plate reader (LPR) technology to over 42 locations across the Southwest border. This deployment will include one fixed LPR facility comparable to inbound processing; five sites with a combination of fixed LPRs and handheld devices; and 36 sites with handheld devices only. In addition, CBP will deploy LPR technology to 20 Border Patrol checkpoints across the SWB for operational integration with both inbound and outbound processing. The deployment of this technology to outbound and checkpoint processing will improve intelligence gathering capabilities and the operational integration of these two processing environments with inbound processing will improve tactical targeting analysis.

Department of Homeland Security, Customs and Border Protection

Program: Office of Air and Marine

Resource Information:

	FY2010 Enacted (000)	FY2012 President's Budget (000)	Delta (FY2012 over FY 2010) (000)
Base Resources	315,581	293,527	(22,054)
Incremental Increase/ Decrease	-	-	-
Program Total	**315,581**	**293,527**	**(22,054)**

Program Description:

Gaining control of the Southwest border involves continuing to improve the U.S. Government's capability to detect, monitor, and respond to the air, land, and maritime threats to the United States. The SWB includes extremely harsh and inhospitable terrain that represents a significant challenge to border security. The Office of Air and Marine (OAM) provides rapid-response surveillance and interdiction capabilities in areas where border enforcement is made difficult due to terrain or location. OAM agents use air and maritime assets to develop and sustain the detection and monitoring, interception, tracking, and apprehension of suspect targets along the Southwest border to guard against illegal activity and border violations on the ground, air, or water. OAM provides air and maritime support to OBP, OFO, and its interagency partners including ICE and the Drug Enforcement Administration (DEA). Within OAM, there are several simultaneous programs that optimize CBP's deterrent and interdiction capabilities along the SWB:

Southwest Operations

The Director of Southwest Operations has overall situational awareness of 23 Aviation and Marine Units located from San Diego, California to Houston, Texas spanning over 2,000 miles of international border. The Director's ongoing mission is to provide its field directors with the correct aviation and maritime assets, personnel, and operational budget to accomplish their missions. The Director has continuous oversight of: aviation operations, training and evaluation of equipment, personnel and asset relocation, administrative, facilities, budgetary, and disciplinary actions occurring within the region. The OBP Sector Chief has tactical control of OAM assets in the Southwest Region and all operations are based on the priorities established by OBP.

Air and Marine Operations Center

The AMOC detects, tracks and coordinates response activities related to suspect aircraft along the Southwest border with other Department of Homeland Security component agencies (U.S. Coast Guard, ICE, and OBP), DoD, El Paso Intelligence Center, and other federal, state, and local authorities, as well as with other interagency task forces and with Mexican authorities. AMOC has historically engaged in close coordination with the Government of Mexico and with Mexican law enforcement personnel.

Recently, the AMOC has developed tracking and intelligence data on SWB ultralight aircraft incursions into the United States.

Information Analysis Center (IAC), Mexico City

OAM has two permanently assigned positions and temporarily assigned personnel at the Information Analysis Center (IAC) at the U.S. Embassy in Mexico City, Mexico. These OAM team members contribute to closer bilateral cooperation with Mexico that holds the potential to reveal more about the air, land, and maritime threats bound for the United States improves our ability to respond to those threats. This center develops actionable intelligence that is shared among the agencies that participate in the program and between the Governments of Mexico and United States.

Unmanned Aircraft System (UAS) Operations

OAM has three UAS operating along the SWB with Unmanned Aircraft System (UAS) flight operations based out of Fort Huachuca, Arizona, and mission control execute from Davis-Monthan AFB, Tucson, Arizona. In FY 2010, while performing border security missions, OAM UAS flew more than 2,511 hours and responded to more than 880 ground sensor activations, 80 of which resulted in the identification of suspected illegal activity such as human or narcotics smuggling. In FY 2011, a new UAS flight operations center was established earlier than planned at the Naval Air Station, Corpus Christi, Texas. Current operations are being funded from OAM base funding. Funds for this site have been requested in the FY 2012 budget. OAM has received Certificate of Authorizations (COA) from the FAA for airspace access for UAS operations from eastern California to the maritime border of Louisiana. These flight hours directly contributed to the seizure of more than 4,242 pounds of narcotics and the apprehension of more than 777 suspects. As UAS operations become more finely integrated into OBP, ICE, and other LE planned targeting efforts along the SWB, the reliance on unattended ground sensors to exclusively cue UAS operations has diminished. The overall reduction of identified suspects and seized narcotics attributed to UAS operations in FY 2010 is reflective of CBP's overall enhanced posture along the SWB and reduced illegal cross-border flow.

Department of Homeland Security, Customs and Border Protection

Program: Border Security Fencing, Infrastructure, and Technology

Resource Information:

		FY2010 Enacted (000)	FY2012 President's Budget (000)	Delta (FY2012 over FY 2010) (000)
Base Resources		76,200	44,550	(31,650)
Incremental Increase/ Decrease		-	-	-
Program Total		**76,200**	**44,550**	**(31,650)**

Program Description:

Beginning in FY 2012, 15 percent of the Border Security Fencing, Infrastructure & Technology (BSFIT) will be considered to be drug related. The BSFIT appropriation supports the DHS border security mission to prevent the illegal flow of people and goods across U.S. air, land, and sea borders while expediting the safe flow of lawful trade and commerce. This appropriation provides continued funding for the following initiatives:

- Establishing and managing comprehensive Tactical Infrastructure (TI) maintenance and repair activities to support fielded pedestrian and vehicle fencing, roads, tower sites, canal crossovers, ongoing vegetation removal and other similar efforts;

- Delivering detection and surveillance technology systems to gain situational awareness of activity at the border, and to provide law enforcement personnel tactical assistance in identifying and resolving illegal activity;

- Modernizing Tactical Communications (TACCOM) systems on the SWB for improved operations and agent safety; and,

- Evaluating emerging technologies and innovative applications of existing technology for broad border security needs.

Reducing the flow of illegal traffic between the ports of entry depends on the appropriate combination of personnel, tactical infrastructure, and technology. Personnel are the most robust and adaptable of these resources, as Border Patrol agents conduct surveillance and respond to incursions. Tactical infrastructure, primarily focused on physical fencing, enhances the ability of personnel to respond by creating delays or by making it easier for agents to reach a particular area.

The Border Patrol primarily uses technology for detection and surveillance between ports of entry, enabling CBP to maximize its effectiveness in responding to and disrupting illicit activity. In other words, technology enhances situational awareness of the amount and types of illegal activity at the border, enabling officers to spend more of their time responding to incursions and less of their time detecting them.

Alternative (Southwest) Border Technologies.

This investment in alternative technologies provides for border surveillance and related technologies prioritized for SWB deployment, and implements initial DHS guidance for refocusing the SBInet program. In January 2010, Secretary Napolitano ordered a quantitative, science-based assessment of CBP's border security technology approach due to concerns over SBInet Block 1 program delays and cost growth. Using the Analysis of Alternatives (AoA), the OBP conducted an operational assessment of border surveillance technology in order to identify the appropriate mix of technologies required to gain situational awareness and manage the Arizona border area. The resultant Arizona technology investment plan is to acquire, deploy, and maintain a mix of agent-related technologies (e.g., night vision binoculars, etc.), mobile surveillance capabilities, integrated fixed tower sensor systems, as well as upgraded Border Patrol command centers with enhanced communications and situational awareness displays. FY 2012 funds will be used to deploy three Integrated Fixed Tower System to Border Patrol stations' areas of responsibility in Arizona.

Development and Deployment funds provide engineering, development, testing, construction and fielding of surveillance and detection technologies, including sensor systems, radars, and day/night cameras to improve the ability of CBP operational forces to detect, identify, classify, and track illegal entries and items of interest (IOIs) across all border environments. These systems are deployed on fixed towers, mobile platforms (wheeled vehicles and aircraft), and through agent portable systems.

Development and Deployment also provides for related activities, such as technical support, systems engineering services; prime contractor program management and systems engineering; advanced technology development, Operational Test & Evaluation support, and environmental planning, assessment and mitigation activities associated with fielding technology and tactical infrastructure.

Department of Homeland Security, Immigration and Customs Enforcement

Program: Homeland Security Investigations (Domestic Investigations)

Resource Information:

	FY2010 Enacted (000)	FY2012 President's Budget (000)	Delta (FY2012 over FY 2010) (000)
Base Resources	159,262	166,346	7,084
Incremental Increase/ Decrease	-	-	-
Program Total	**159,262**	**166,346**	**7,084**

Program Description:

ICE Homeland Security Investigations (HSI) conducts the critical function of investigations. In support of the SWB CN Strategy, ICE HSI investigates illicit activities, such as: weapons smuggling, bulk cash smuggling, narcotrafficking and money laundering. ICE HSI has several components that focus on investigations that have an impact upon domestic, intelligence and international areas.

ICE HSI houses the BEST initiative. The BEST is comprised of Federal, state, local and international law enforcement agencies. The resources of these law enforcement agencies provide a comprehensive approach in the identifying, targeting and dismantling of cross-border criminal organizations involved in drug and weapons trafficking and money laundering. This task force is designed to enhance information sharing between participating organizations and to foster a collaborative environment in investigative efforts. BESTs provide a unified and international response to securing our borders, stemming the violence, and assisting first responders.

The BEST initiative parlays the skills sets and best practices of its partner agencies in the following:

- Gathering, analyzing, data mining and sharing of intelligence;

- Interdicting contraband, weapons and bulk cash entering and exiting the U.S. illegally; and

- Identifying, disrupting, dismantling and prosecuting cross-border smuggling and trafficking organizations.

ICE partners with CBP on combating transnational criminal networks smuggling weapons into Mexico from the United States. As part of this initiative, the United States and the Government of Mexico agreed to bi-lateral interdiction, investigation, and intelligence-sharing activities to identify, disrupt, and dismantle these networks engaged in weapons smuggling. On this front, ICE will coordinate with the Bureau of Alcohol, Tobacco, Firearms and Explosives' (ATF) Project Gunrunner.

Financial Investigations

To augment investigations along the SWB, ICE/HSI focuses its financial investigations program on crimes associated with national security and critical infrastructure. ICE/HSI aggressively pursues the financial component of every investigation and supports many long-standing initiatives to minimize threats to national security, such as money laundering, bulk cash smuggling, unlicensed money service businesses, and corrupt foreign officials. ICE is the primary investigative agency with jurisdiction over bulk cash smuggling crimes.

Counter Proliferation Investigations (CPI)

As the investigation arm of DHS, ICE responds to and supports the task of investigating the illegal smuggling of weapons from the U.S. into Mexico. In FY 2010, ICE in partnership with Federal, state, and international law enforcement officials expanded its ongoing Border Crimes Initiative to include the creation of BESTs in five locations along the SWB.

The Counter-Proliferations Unit (CPIU) at HSI headquarters is responsible for developing and implementing national policies and programs in support of the U.S.'s export control regime. The CPIU has long served a significant role in interdicting the illicit flow of weapons and ammunition to Mexico through its support of BESTs in the field. Specifically, CPIU supports the BEST program in two ways: the National Export Enforcement Coordination Network (NEECN) and the Exodus Command Center (ECC). The NEECN supports field agents by working with other federal agencies in the Washington, DC area to both coordinate and de-conflict criminal investigations. One of the elements of a violation under 22 U.S.C. § 2778 is when a target exports a licensable item from the U.S. and fails to obtain an export license for that item. The ECC is the sole conduit between DHS personnel in the field and the licensing agencies in Washington, DC to obtain that evidence for use in criminal prosecution.

Department of Homeland Security, Immigration and Customs Enforcement

Program: Office of Intelligence

Resource Information:

	FY2010 Enacted (000)	FY2012 President's Budget (000)	Delta (FY2012 over FY 2010) (000)
Base Resources	6,906	7,225	319
Incremental Increase/ Decrease	-	-	-
Program Total	**6,906**	**7,225**	**319**

Program Description:

ICE HSI Intelligence program includes Intelligence Officers, Research Analysts, and Reports Officers at existing SWB Field Intelligence Groups and at current BESTs along the SWB. These Field Intelligence Groups support ICE's capability to develop preoperational intelligence reports, strategic intelligence products, and post-operational impact assessments. These products will enable the enforcement resources of the DHS, ICE, and partner agencies to have the maximum impact possible to protect the Homeland, stem SWB violence, and uphold public safety. Additionally, ICE HSI intelligence support includes the following: collaboration with agencies within the Intelligence Community, document exploitation capabilities for ICE field offices, trend and pattern analysis used to build forecast models, and the ability to inform the overall enforcement focus along the SWB on law enforcement execution and vital resource management issues.

The Report Writers Program helps ensure that information collected by ICE is appropriately shared with the Intelligence Community. ICE's information can fill gaps in intelligence reporting and enable the United States to uncover previously unknown connections among terrorist organizations or other criminal groups. Proper reporting, which includes recognition of the source of the information, serves to promote secure borders by integrating domestic, border, and international intelligence.

Department of Homeland Security, Immigration and Customs Enforcement

Program: Office of International Affairs (International Investigations)

Resource Information:

	FY2010 Enacted (000)	FY2012 President's Budget (000)	Delta (FY2012 over FY 2010) (000)
Base Resources	1,465	2,060	595
Incremental Increase/ Decrease	-	-	-
Program Total	**1,465**	**2,060**	**595**

Program Description:

In support of the *Southwest Border Counternarcotics Strategy*, ICE/International Affairs (IA) provides law enforcement support and functionality to facilitate criminal investigations into violations of immigration and customs laws. The strategic placement of ICE personnel promotes more aggressive host-country law enforcement operations and can provide capacity building to host-country law enforcement organizations. ICE/IA identifies criminal activities and eliminates vulnerabilities that threaten the United States, as well as enforce economic, transportation and infrastructure security. Strategically, ICE's vision is to marginalize the impact of Mexico-based criminal organizations through prevention and deterrence efforts that engage these criminals at points of genesis or vulnerability rather than points of access, such as the U.S.-Mexico border.

ICE's investigative priorities in its foreign offices include among others preventing weapons and bulk cash smuggling, money laundering, and narcotrafficking. As ICE/IA engages in bilateral interdiction, investigation and intelligence-sharing activities with international partners, cross-border criminal networks engaged in the smuggling and trafficking of weapons, aliens and contraband are disrupted and dismantled.

Department of the Interior

Components within the Department of the Interior participate in counterdrug activities along the SWB. Although funding cannot accurately be estimated at this time, activities along the SWB are listed below.

Bureau of Indian Affairs (BIA)

The BIA's Office of Justice Services (OJS) provides for the safety of Indian communities by ensuring the protection of life and property, enforcing laws, and maintaining justice and order. SWB funding supports law enforcement officers who address illegal smuggling of drugs and immigrants on reservations on or near the Mexican border. These officers assist the Department in meeting its strategic plan goal of reducing the number of serious offenses that occur on Interior lands and reducing the number of injuries to visitors. The additional law enforcement personnel along the border decreases criminal activity and helps prevent the destruction of priceless natural and cultural resources.

National Park Service (NPS)

The NPS utilizes law enforcement park rangers, special agents and other Federal, state, and local law enforcement authorities and organizations to assist in providing security and protection of park resources and ensuring visitor safety on park lands adjacent to international borders. Ongoing efforts at these parks include ranger patrols and surveillance of roads, trails, and backcountry areas; construction of barricades to prevent illegal vehicle traffic; short and long-term counter-smuggling and drug cultivation investigations and operations. NPS staff also implements projects to mitigate environmental damage caused by illegal activities.

Department of Justice, U.S. Marshals Service

Program: Southwest Border Activities

Resource Information:

	FY2010 Enacted (000)	FY2012 President's Budget (000)	Delta (FY2012 over FY 2010) (000)
Base Resources	25,858	33,195	7,337
Incremental Increase/ Decrease	16,561	10,927	(5,634)
Program Total	**42,419**	**44,122**	**1,073**

Program Description:

The U.S. Marshals Service supports the *Strategy* through fugitive apprehension and prisoner handling. As of March 2011, the five USMS SWB districts had 5,968 prisoners in custody who were charged with drug-related offenses. This represents 24.5% of the total prisoner population along the SWB. USMS personnel in Mexico City will work with their Mexican counterparts to target both foreign and international fugitives believed to be in Mexico, and the USMS will continue to encourage participation in its international law enforcement training programs for Mexican law enforcement personnel.

Department of Justice, Drug Enforcement Administration

Program: DEA Southwest Border and Mexico Resources

Resource Information:

	FY2010 Enacted (000)	FY2012 President's Budget (000)	Delta (FY2012 over FY 2010) (000)
Base Resources	347,486	410,483	62,997
Incremental Increase/Decrease	25,575	(2,140)	(27,715)
Program Total	**373,061**	**408,343**	**35,282**

Program Description:

DEA has several operational efforts targeting Mexican drug trafficking cartels operating along the SWB to disrupt the drug transportation infrastructure. Initiatives that contribute to DEA's effort along the SWB include:

- The Southwest Border Intelligence Collection Plan (SWBICP) provides a regional intelligence collection framework to support enforcement operations on the Southwest border of the United States. Intelligence gathered under the guidance of the SWBICP is shared with the Intelligence Community (IC) and other Federal, state, and local law enforcement agencies. The SWBICP also provides a mechanism to collect information needed to assess counterdrug activity and security along the U.S.–Mexico border.

- The License Plate Reader (LPR) Initiative along the SWB uses various technologies to read vehicle license plates with photographic imaging equipment. The LPR Initiative combines existing DEA and other law enforcement database capabilities with new technology to identify and interdict conveyances being utilized to transport bulk cash, drugs, weapons, as well as other illegal contraband.

- DEA is an active component of the Organized Crime and Drug Enforcement Task Forces (OCDETF) program, including OCDETF Strike Forces that collaborate with the SWB HIDTA regional task forces that represent Federal, state, and local partnerships targeting Mexican drug cartels and their smuggling and transportation networks that spawn cartel violence along the border.

- The Southwest Border Initiative is a multi-agency, Federal law enforcement operation that attacks Mexico-based DTOs operating along the SWB by targeting the communication systems of their command and control centers. As part of a cooperative effort, DEA, Federal Bureau of Investigation (FBI), CBP, and the U.S. Attorneys' Offices around the country conduct communication intercepts that ultimately identify all levels of Mexico or Colombia-based DTOs.

- DEA is a member of the BEST, an ICE-led multi-agency initiative designed to increase the flow of information between participating agencies regarding violent criminal organizations and gangs operating in and around Laredo, Texas. In addition, BEST targets human and violent drug smuggling organizations that fuel violence in the Laredo, TX area.

EPIC is a national tactical and strategic intelligence center that supports law enforcement efforts throughout the Western Hemisphere, and it is DEA's long-standing and most important intelligence sharing organization focusing on the SWB. EPIC provides immediate access to participating agencies' databases to law enforcement agents, investigators, and analysts at all levels of government, throughout the U.S. and with some foreign nations. EPIC also provides significant, direct tactical intelligence support to state and local law enforcement agencies, especially in the areas of clandestine laboratory investigations and highway interdiction efforts.

EPIC's Gatekeeper Project is a comprehensive, multi-source assessment of trafficking organizations involved in and controlling the movement of illegal contraband through "entry corridors" along the Southwest border. The analysis of Gatekeeper organizations serves as a guide for policymakers to initiate enforcement operations and prioritize operations by U.S. anti-drug elements. Numerous Gatekeepers have direct links to Priority Target Organizations and/or Consolidated Priority Organization Targets.

The SWB is part of DEA's larger Drug Flow Attack Strategy (DFAS) in the Western Hemisphere. DFAS is an innovative, multi-agency strategy designed to significantly disrupt the flow of drugs, money, and chemicals between the source zones and the U.S. by attacking vulnerabilities in the supply chains, transportation systems, and financial infrastructure of major DTOs.

Department of Justice, Interagency Crime Drug Enforcement

Program: Organized Crime Drug Enforcement Task Force

Resource Information:

	FY2010 Enacted (000)	FY2012 President's Budget (000)	Delta (FY2012 over FY 2010) (000)
Base Resources	135,380	137,183	1,803
Incremental Increase/ Decrease	21,000	9,300	(11,700)
Program Total	**156,380**	**146,483**	**(9,897)**

Program Description:

All OCDETF SWB-related cases are conducted by prosecutor-led multi-agency task forces. OCDETF uses its resources to support the investigative activities of the following participating agencies: ATF, DEA, FBI, and USMS along the Southwest border. It also utilizes its reimbursable prosecution resources situated at the 93 U.S. Attorneys' Offices around the country (executed through the Executive Office for U.S. Attorneys) and at the Criminal Division of the Department of Justice (executed through attorneys in the Criminal Division and the OCDETF Executive Office) for SWB prosecutorial activities. Approximately 42% of OCDETF investigations are SWB-related, while 40% of its defendants also come from cases related to this region.

OCDETF combines the resources and expertise of its seven Federal agency members—the DEA; the FBI; the ATF; the USMS; the Internal Revenue Service (IRS); ICE; and the USCG—in cooperation with the Department of Justice's Criminal Division, the 93 U.S. Attorneys' Offices, and state and local law enforcement, to identify, disrupt, and dismantle the drug trafficking and money laundering organizations most responsible for the Nation's supply of illegal drugs and the violence the drug trade generates and fuels. The OCDETF Fusion Center (OFC) is a comprehensive data center containing all drug and related financial intelligence information from all seven OCDETF-member investigative agencies, and the Financial Crimes Enforcement Network as well as relevant data from many other agencies. The OFC is designed to conduct cross-agency integration and analysis of the data, create comprehensive intelligence pictures of targeted organizations, including those identified as Consolidated Priority Organization Targets and Regional Priority Organization Targets, and pass actionable leads through the multi-agency Special Operations Division to OCDETF participants in the field including the OCDETF Co-located Strike Forces.

Department of Justice, Office of the Federal Detention Trustee

Program: Southwest Border Detention Activities

Resource Information:

	FY2010 Enacted (000)	FY2012 President's Budget (000)	Delta (FY2012 over FY 2010) (000)
Base Resources	139,949	179,721	39,772
Incremental Increase/ Decrease	11,551	(14,257)	(25,808)
Program Total	**151,500**	**165,464**	**13,964**

Program Description:

The Office of the Federal Detention Trustee (OFDT) provides funding to the USMS to support housing for persons arrested along the SWB and detained while awaiting trial. For FY 2010, SWB drug-related resources were $151.5 million and 6,400 average daily population (ADP). For FY 2012, SWB drug-related resources were $165.5 million and 6,011 ADP. In FY 2012, anticipated law enforcement initiatives on the SWB that address drug and weapons trafficking is expected to increase the average time-in-detention, which would increase the cost.

The Criminal Division and United States Attorneys' Office also participate in counterdrug activities along the southwest border. However, at this time, neither component has a data system in place to accurately capture funding dedicated to the region. A summary of their activities along the southwest border is below.

Criminal Division

The Criminal Division (CRM) develops, enforces, and supervises the application of all Federal criminal laws, except those specifically assigned to other divisions. The Division and the 93 U.S. Attorneys are responsible for overseeing criminal matters under more than 900 statutes, as well as certain civil litigation. CRM supervises a wide range of criminal investigations and prosecutions, including international and national drug trafficking and money laundering organizations; international organized crime groups; and corrupt public officials. The Criminal Division prosecutors investigate and prosecute the most threatening drug traffickers in the SWB region. To combat the substantial threat of violence posed by these narcotics trafficking groups, the Division works with U.S. and Mexican Federal, state, and local law enforcement and criminal justice authorities to develop and implement law enforcement initiatives aimed at reducing the escalating drug-related violence along the U.S.—Mexico border.

- The Division, through its Gang Unit, investigates and prosecutes regional, national and international gangs, including activities along the SWB.

- The Human Rights and Special Prosecutions Section (HRSP) secures the borders by enforcing Federal criminal laws relating to alien smuggling and other immigration-related offenses.

- The Division's Asset Forfeiture and Money Laundering Section (AFMLS) prosecutes and coordinates complex, sensitive, multi-district, and international money laundering and asset forfeiture investigations and cases. AFMLS' Mexican Drug Cartel Team works with the U.S. Attorneys' Offices, including those at the SWB, and other litigation components, to strip the financial base from the major drug trafficking and money laundering organizations. Once fully implemented, the Department will litigate asset recovery cases on behalf of countries victimized by high-level corruption, including corruption fueled by drug trafficking organizations. Lastly, AFMLS, in conjunction with the Organized Crime and Drug Enforcement Task Forces (OCDETF), is the sole provider of specialized financial investigations training, which provides investigators and prosecutors the necessary skills to trace money internationally and make money laundering charging decisions in international drug cases.

- The Office of Enforcement Operations' Wiretap Unit provides direct operational support to the U.S. Attorneys' Offices, other Federal prosecutors, and agents by reviewing all applications for electronic surveillance and by providing guidance to agents and prosecutors on the justification for the development of such applications.

- The Office of International Affairs (OIA) serves as the U.S. Central Authority for all formal requests for mutual legal assistance and all requests for extradition. Virtually all SWB enforcement initiatives (Federal and state) will, at some stage, be working directly with OIA to obtain critical evidence and fugitives located in Mexico and elsewhere. In addition, Mexico will continue to need formal assistance in dealing with fugitives and evidence in its investigations.

- The Division has the sole responsibility in reviewing all cases using Racketeer Influenced and Corrupt Organizations Statute (RICO). The RICO Statute is a critical and powerful tool used to dismantle entire criminal organizations, including drug cartels. As smaller gangs and drug traffickers gradually build into larger, much more dangerous and large-scale organized criminal organizations, there is an increased use of the RICO Statute in order to address these groups as a whole, as opposed to each individual member.

- Corruption of U.S. customs and border officials can undermine the integrity of our borders and threaten our national security. The Public Integrity Section (PIN) spearheads the Department's national effort to combat corruption, and is coordinating with the FBI and other investigative agencies in the Border Corruption Task Force.

Department of State, Bureau of International Narcotics and Law Enforcement Affairs

Program: Merida Initiative (Mexico)

Resource Information:

	FY2010 Estimate (000)	FY2012 President's Budget (000)	Delta (FY2012 over FY 2010) (000)
Base Resources			
INCLE	284,000	248,500	(35,500)
ESF	9,000	33,260	24,260
Incremental Increase/ Decrease	-	-	-
Program Total	**293,000**	**281,760**	**(11,240)**

Note: a) FY 2010 includes $354 million of FY 2009 Supplemental funds, which includes $94 million in INCLE. b) Since both the Central America Regional Security Initiative and the Caribbean Basin Security Initiative are not included in the 2011 *Southwest Border Counternarcotics Strategy*, the Resource Annex doesn't capture the funding information of those initiatives.

Program Description:

In order to tackle the immediate security challenges faced by the Government of Mexico and the national security implications for the U.S., the overall objectives of the assistance are to break the power and impunity of criminal organizations; strengthen border, air, and maritime controls; improve the capacity of justice systems in the region to conduct investigations and prosecutions; consolidate the rule of law, protect human rights, and reform prison management; curtail criminal gang activity; and reduce the demand for drugs throughout the region. In FY 2011, the budget will mark the transition within the Merida Initiative from equipment support toward the implementation of a long-term bilateral program focused on training and technical assistance to implement comprehensive justice sector reform.

International Narcotics Control and Law Enforcement (INCLE) ($248.5 million, FY 2012 request)

The U.S. will provide training and technical assistance to Federal, state, and local law enforcement and interdiction activities, as well as expand vetted units and improve operational development and integrity, to disrupt the organized criminal groups. Funding will also support the proposed reform of the justice sector (including the expansion of an accusatorial system and the reform of Mexico's code of criminal procedure) and provide training and technical assistance to the broad range of justice sector-related personnel to ensure effective prosecutions. Border surveillance and control will be strengthened through training, and technical assistance. Programs will also encourage the creation and implementation of demand-reduction strategies and the promotion of the rule of law.

Economic Support Funds (ESF) ($33.3 million, FY 2012 request)

The U.S. will continue to play a vital role in advancing rule of law by promoting the implementation of the new criminal justice system. Support will be provided for federal and state justice systems as they transition from a written inquisitorial system of justice to an oral accusatorial system, as required by the 2008 constitutional reforms. Cooperation on reducing corruption and advancing human rights will remain central themes of U.S. assistance to Mexico. The U.S. will continue to provide technical assistance to justice sector personnel in the drafting and implementing of oral adversarial codes of criminal procedure. The U.S. will also support community crime prevention initiatives aimed at addressing the underlying causes of crime and violence, and will help build community capacity to resist crime and effectively collaborate with institutions and law enforcement-based security efforts.

Appendix C: Common Abbreviations

ALPR	Automated License Plate Reader
AMOC	Air and Marine Operations Center
ASTI	Arms and Strategic Technology Investigations
ATF	Bureau of Alcohol, Tobacco, Firearms and Explosives
BEST	Border Enforcement Security Task Force
BIA	Bureau of Indian Affairs
BIFS	Border Intelligence Fusion Center
BLM	Bureau of Land Management
BLO	Border Liaison Officer
BVIC	Border Violence Intelligence Cell
CAFÉ	Central American Fingerprint Exchange
CBP	U.S. Customs and Border Protection
CBP A&M	U.S. Customs and Border Protection Air and Marine
CBP/OFO	U.S. Customs and Border Protection/Office of Field Operations
CCDB	Consolidated Counterdrug Database
CIFTA	Inter-American Convention Against the Illicit Manufacturing of and Trafficking in Firearms, Ammunition, Explosives, and Other Related Materials (1997)
CONOPS	Concept of Operations
COP	Common Operating Picture
CPOT	Consolidated Priority Organization Target
CTAC	Counterdrug Technology Assessment Center
DDTC	Directorate of Defense Trade Controls
DEA	Drug Enforcement Administration
DFAS	Drug Flow Attack Strategy
DHS/S&T	Department of Homeland Security/Directorate for Science and Technology
DOD	Department of Defense
DOI	Department of the Interior

DOJ	Department of Justice
DOS	Department of State
EPIC	El Paso Intelligence Center
ERDC	U.S. Army Engineer Research and Development Center
FBI	Federal Bureau of Investigation
FDL	Forensic Document Laboratory
FEMA	Federal Emergency Management Agency
FFL	Federal Firearms Licensee
FinCEN	Financial Crimes Enforcement Network
FTE	Full Time Equivalent
GCA	Gun Control Act of 1968
HIDTA	High Intensity Drug Trafficking Areas
HSI Intel	Homeland Security Investigations Intelligence (ICE)
HSTC	Human Smuggling and Trafficking Center
IAFIS	Integrated Automated Fingerprint Identification System
IBIS	Integrated Ballistic Identification System
ICE	U.S. Immigration and Customs Enforcement
ICE/HSI	U.S. Immigration and Customs Enforcement/Homeland Security Investigations
ICE/HSI/OIA	U.S. Immigration and Customs Enforcement /Homeland Security Investigations/Office of International Affairs
IDBF	Identity and Benefit Fraud
IDENT	Automated Biometrics Identification System
IRS	Internal Revenue Service
IWG-IC	Interagency Working Group on Intelligence Coordination
JCTD	Joint Capability Technology Demonstration
JIATF-S	Joint Interagency Task Force South
JTF North	Joint Task Force North
JTTR	Joint Tunnel Testing Range
MOU	Memorandum of Understanding
MSB	Money Services Business

NDDS	U.S. Department of Justice Narcotic and Dangerous Drug Section
NDIC	National Drug Intelligence Center
NIBIN	National Integrated Ballistics Information Network
NPS	National Park Service
NSS	National Seizure System
NTC	National Targeting Center—Passenger
NTC-C	National Targeting Center—Cargo
OCDETF	Organized Crime Drug Enforcement Task Force
OFAC	Office of Foreign Assets Control
OFC	OCDETF Fusion Center
OFDT	Office of the Federal Detention Trustee
ONDCP	Office of National Drug Control Policy
OPDAT	Office of Overseas Prosecutorial Development, Assistance and Training
ORDCP	Other-Related Drug Control Program
POE	Port of Entry
PRIDE	Port Radiation Inspection, Detection, and Evaluation
RAID	Real-Time Analytical Intelligence Database
RPOT	Regional Priority Organization Target
SDTF	San Diego Tunnel Task Force
SIPRNET	Secret Internet Protocol Router Network
SOD	Special Operations Division
STRAP	Surveillance and Tracking Radar Processor
SURGE	Specialized Urban Response Gang Enforcement
SWIG	Southwest Intelligence Group
TAG	Transnational Anti-Gang
TARS	Tethered Aerostat Radar System
TECS	formerly the Treasury Enforcement Communications System
TIC	The Interdiction Committee
UIF	Unidad de Inteligencia Financiera (Mexico)
USCG	United States Coast Guard

USCG/ICC	United States Coast Guard/ Intelligence Coordination Center
USDA	United States Department of Agriculture
USFS	United States Forest Service
USFWS	United States Fish and Wildlife Service
USMS	U.S. Marshals Service
USMS/TOG	U.S. Marshals Service Tactical Operations Group
USNORTHCOM	United States Northern Command
US-VISIT	United States Visitor and Immigrant Status Indicator Technology
VCIT	Violent Crime Impact Team
WVTF	Weapons Virtual Task Force